PILGRIM

ONE THOUSAND DAYS ON THE ROAD

PILGRIM
ONE THOUSAND DAYS ON THE ROAD

REFLECTIONS FOR THE BUSINESS TRAVELER

LUIS FERNANDO
ARAGÓN

WinePressPublishing
Your Book, Defined. Since 1991.

WinePress Publishing (PO Box 428, Enumclaw, WA 98022) functions only as book publisher. As such, the ultimate design, content, editorial accuracy, and views expressed or implied in this work are those of the author.

Unless otherwise noted, all Scriptures are taken from the *Holy Bible, New International Version®, NIV®*. Copyright © 1973, 1978, 1984 by Biblica, Inc.™ Used by permission of Zondervan. All rights reserved worldwide. www.zondervan. com

ISBN 13: 978-1-4141-1737-9
ISBN 10: 1-4141-1737-X
Library of Congress Catalog Card Number: 2010902841

CONTENTS

INTRODUCTION

TRAVEL POSES MANY challenges, but my intention in this book is not to deal with how travelers can avoid discomfort or how they can think happy thoughts in the midst of a difficult journey. I am not even interested in the traveler's need to avoid being robbed or to be protected from so many of the other physical dangers and challenges that are so real on the road. Instead, this book deals with the trials we face as Christians—trials not unlike those faced every day at home, and yet trials that can be more difficult to overcome on the road.

They call us "Road Warriors." How romantic, how exciting ...how stupid. The euphemism doesn't stop there. A Courtyard by Marriott advertisement reads, "Toting briefcases and carrying barely carry-onable luggage through a hundred airports. It's enough to make a business traveler tough as nails." The advertisement is meant to make us feel like heroes; like some special breed of brave soldiers. In truth, what we are is hundreds of thousands of tired, stressed-out men and women who face too many problems every day.

How we deal with trials during travel is important, because a business traveler, like a pilgrim, has a very specific purpose, a clear destination and a goal. Unlike a tourist, however, a pilgrim's purpose is beyond the journey itself: traveling is not enough, no matter in how much style it is done. How each trip is handled will ultimately determine whether its specific goal is achieved. How trips as a whole are approached can also determine whether our final goal is achieved, be it financial stability, a beautiful family, or eternal life.

The point is that when we are distracted with frequent business travel, our salvation and spiritual health could be put at risk. The dangers of conformity, the tedium of normality, or the temptation of despair all put us at risk. At one point we may be slipping slowly down a path of petty sins and general apathy that erode our souls, while at another point we may be struggling with the devastation of insignificance or with the frustration of failing in the most basic things in our attempts to accomplish great goals for Christ. Among other things, in the light of Paul's words in Ephesians 6:12 about waging a spiritual war, this book tells how I have won many battles while acknowledging that I have lost my share.

Being on the road is a helpful, constant reminder that we are only pilgrims on this earth. We dwell in temporary homes, always trying to adjust to the surroundings, always striving for that elusive comfort, while we secretly—perhaps even unconsciously—long for our heavenly home, the only place where we truly belong.

I have organized my thousand days on the road into forty journeys or stories, inspired by Christian tradition and those passages in the Bible in which forty days are seen as a time of preparation or a time of trial, prayer or fasting before something great happens. Genesis 7–8 tells us about the forty days and forty nights of rain in the great flood; Exodus 24 and 34 tell us how Moses (on two separate occasions) climbed Mount Sinai and spent forty days and forty nights alone with God; 1 Kings 19:8 tells us how Elijah fled and prayed for God to take his life, but God fed him and strengthened him so that he could take on a forty-day journey to mount Horeb; and Luke 4:1-13 tells us how Jesus Himself was led into the desert by the Holy Spirit, where He fasted for forty days and was tempted by the Devil. Forty was also the number of years that God led His people in the desert to humble them and test them in order to know what was in their hearts (see Deuteronomy 8:2). Forty are the stories in this book.

Why should you read this book? Why did I get it published? After all, I am no theologian or philosopher. I simply try to use my intelligence and my senses to look at the world around me and understand life, with the help of God's Word. You probably do the same thing. I am no poet, although my ability to paint a picture with words is fortunately better than my ability to draw with a pencil.

I am definitely not a saint either, but I try to follow James's instruction to not only listen to the Word but also put it into practice (see James 1:22)—oftentimes with disappointing results. I am the kind of man who can read the Bible at six a.m. on an airplane and be deeply inspired by reading how Jesus, after being told that His cousin and close friend John the Baptist had been beheaded, tried to get away to pray but was met by a large crowd with many needs. He set aside His own grief, healed their sick, and then provided for them to eat. Not until He had taken care of all their needs did He spend some time alone in prayer, as He had intended to do (see Matthew 14:12-16). At 6:30 a.m. I can pray to God for the type of love that selflessly cares for others, only to throw it all out the window when I get home in the evening and tell my dear wife, Ana María, that I don't want to hear about her frustrations with our children because I had a long day and am too tired. I still have a *long* way to go.

I know that I am a son of God through the precious blood of Jesus Christ. I am also a fighter; I strive to stand my ground and, after I have done everything, hope that I may stand. I know that it is God's grace that will see me through, but I also want to do everything I can to please Him. The stories in this book tell of a traveler's honest search for righteousness—nothing outstanding, nothing special. God has called a few ordinary people to do some extraordinary things; the vast majority of us will remain extraordinary wannabes who are called to take care of all the ordinary things. Walking in Jesus' footsteps in humble obedience is challenging enough for me.

I am a husband and father of two (Ana María and I were married in 1988). I am an exercise scientist; someone who loves sports and underwent ten years of higher education to find out how little we know about human physiology and sports nutrition. I live in Costa Rica, teach at the University of Costa Rica, and have spent a sizable amount of time (more than ninety days each year) traveling internationally during eleven full years of working as a consultant. To some of you, that hardly qualifies as a Road Warrior, but I have done my share of work-related travel.

This is not a book about wonderful, outstanding stories. In fact, when my wife read the first few sections, she said, "This is really not what I expected. I had misunderstood you. I thought you were going to share special stories and how God had listened to your prayers in miraculous ways during your trips." Well, she had misunderstood me indeed, although I know that God has listened to my prayers during my trips. In this book, I want to share my reflections, my struggles and my insights in the hope that you may be inspired by some of them.

> *A Christian and an unbelieving poet may both be equally original in the sense that they neglect the example of their poetic forbears and draw on resources peculiar to themselves, but with this difference. The unbeliever may take his own temperament and experience, just as they happen to stand, and consider them worth communicating simply because they are facts or, worse still, because they are his. To the Christian his own temperament and experience, as mere fact, and as merely his, are of no value or importance whatsoever: he will deal with them, if at all, only because they are the medium through which, or the position from which, something universally profitable appeared to him.*
> —C. S. Lewis, *Christianity and Literature*

A PLACE TO LIVE

AS A ROAD Warrior, you have your preferences. You have learned from experience to avoid a room that is right in front of the elevator, or next to it, because of the traffic and accompanying noise. For the same reason, you stay away from ice machines (it seems that people always need ice when you are sleeping). Social areas are meant for, well, socializing, which normally involves lower to intolerable levels of noise; by definition, if you are in your room you are not trying to socialize, and hence those areas do not mix well with rooms. Why would a hotel place them next to each other?

Noise from car traffic in parking lots and city streets is compounded by the high probability of a car alarm going off in the middle of the night. You may cringe at the sight of a connecting door between your room and the next one, because you know that even though you may keep it locked to avoid connecting with your neighbor, you will end up sharing his or her choices of TV channels and perhaps even hear him or her singing in the shower. You worry if you forget to check to make sure the connecting door is locked, as you wouldn't want your neighbor to check out your room while you were away or, even worse, while you were asleep.

What is worse than getting a small room with no view? Getting a small room with no view *next to a suite*. I had arrived a couple hours earlier and, for a change, had unpacked all my belongings in anticipation of a five-night stay for a conference. Then my next-door neighbors arrived. "Wow, do you see this?" I heard them say. "Check this out. This place is awesome!" Envy corroded me as I heard them touring their suite. This was swiftly followed by fear when I heard one of them talking on the telephone to a friend. "Joe, guess what?" the voice said. "We got a suite. You wouldn't believe it. Come check it out!" As the guests began arriving with chips, beer, music, whatever, the despair settled in. I couldn't believe how many people these guys knew. Two hours later, I had packed my bags and requested to be transferred to another room.

I know what you're thinking, but I am not picky. It's just that I need my sleep when I travel, even more than when I'm at home. Seriously, I am not picky. After all, my favorite hotel for business travel is the Holiday Inn Express in Palatine, Illinois. My co-workers tease me about this, because the hotel is not particularly fancy; there is no restaurant on the premises, and while the fitness facility is large and convenient, it is a bit spartan. But I know exactly what to expect the three or four times I stay there each year when I visit the Gatorade® Sports Science Institute (GSSI) headquarters in Barrington. I am greeted upon arrival with a "welcome back, Mr. Aragon." I feel at home.

> Do not let your hearts be troubled. Trust in God; trust also in me. In my Father's house are many rooms; if it were not so, I would have told you. I am going there to prepare a place for you. And if I go and prepare a place for you, I will come back and take you to be with me that you also may be where I am. You know the way to the place where I am going.
> —John 14:1-4

I don't know about you, but I resent travel. I don't like to be away from home. God has placed in my heart a strong desire for His heavenly home, and I am particularly aware of my pilgrim condition both on this earth in everyday life as well as during travel. This is especially true when there are clear contrasts in the place I am staying, such as when I visited the Hudson Hotel in New York City. I had arrived there after a six-hour delay on Sunday, June 5, 2005, for a three-day business meeting. My first impression of the hotel was "dark": the lobby was dark, the elevators were dark, and the hallways were extremely dark.

"It's trendy," my colleagues said.

"Dark is dark," I replied.

Then came the room: it was small. It was *really* small. I couldn't believe how small it was. And at $327 a night, it felt even smaller. I checked the room service menu and found that the prices were in line with the room's price. (Fearing that the portions would also be in proportion to the size of the room, I chose to go out instead.) Even knowing that New York was an expensive place, I felt cheated. I longed for home.

> *He who was seated on the throne said, "I am making everything new!" Then he said, "Write this down, for these words are trustworthy and true." He said to me: "It is done. I am the Alpha and the Omega, the Beginning and the End. To him who is thirsty I will give to drink without cost from the spring of the water of life. He who overcomes will inherit all this, and I will be his God and he will be my son."*
> —Revelation 21:5-7

On that day we will finally be home and receive what is ours by the infinite grace of God. We will be in a place that Christ Himself has prepared for us in His Father's mansion.

TRIATHLON AND PRIORITIES

B ACK IN 1985, when I was a single and young assistant professor at the University of Costa Rica, I was invited by the government of Japan for a ten-day visit of Tokyo and Kyoto on the occasion of International Youth Year. The invitation was a total surprise, and it looked like a wonderful opportunity, complete with all expenses covered. As is the case with most great opportunities, I had to make a quick decision.

I decided to accept the invitation. After all, I could get a colleague to cover my classes in my absence, and I could certainly continue to train for the El Coco Triathlon, which was only a few weeks away, during the trip. Well, I knew the cycling would be a problem, but I thought that I would be able to find a lap pool at my hotel, and running could be done anywhere.... This was an opportunity I could not miss, even though I had been training for El Coco for several months.

I was not ready for the challenges I faced: a change in diet, absolute jet lag, a packed agenda, distractions and entertainment, work pressures. It soon became clear that I would have to focus on the running and forget the rest—and with the rest went my prayer times.

A few days after my return to Costa Rica, I went to church on Sunday evening. Fr. Fernando Muñoz was preaching the gospel with great inspiration, and he touched my heart. He preached about loving God and about setting your priorities straight. I painfully realized that my priorities had not been right: by choosing to travel to Japan, I had decided that El Coco was not that important, when it really was. But worse, by focusing on running and not praying, I had decided that El Coco was more important than my relationship with God.

That night I repented, and I decided not to compete in the El Coco Triathlon as a personal sign that from that day forward God was to be my number one priority.

> *One of the teachers of the law came and heard them debating. Noticing that Jesus had given them a good answer, he asked him, "Of all the commandments, which is the most important?" "The most important one," answered Jesus, "is this: 'Hear, O Israel, the Lord our God, the Lord is one. Love the Lord your God with all your heart and with all your soul and with all your mind and with all your strength.'"*
>
> —Mark 12:28-30

NO ROOM FOR US

I HAVE TO admit that my flight delay was nothing compared to the complications suffered by those who endured the 250 or so cancellations due to luggage handling problems at the brand-new Heathrow 5 terminal in March 2008. It was nothing compared to the delays suffered by the passengers of the more than 2,500 American Airlines flights that had to be cancelled on that nightmare week in April 2008. And it was just a minor inconvenience compared to the complications, uncertainty, and sheer terror experienced by passengers flying to U.S. airports on September 11, 2001, who were diverted to other airports and got stuck there for several days.

In my particular case, it was July 1998, and I was flying to Durango, Colorado, for a scientific meeting. I was bringing my wife and eight-year-old daughter with me, and we were all excited to travel together. Earlier that day, our airline's central passenger control system for boarding passes had crashed. At the time, we were not aware of the seriousness of the problem—to us, it simply meant that our first flight of the day would leave a couple hours late. Our late departure was complicated further when the pilot announced that we would have to make a stop in Guatemala City, Guatemala, because we did not have enough fuel on board (?). This meant spending two hours on board on the ground before continuing to the U.S. We flew into Dallas/Ft. Worth International Airport and, after being told that we would *definitely* not make it to our final destination that day, were put on a flight to Albuquerque, New Mexico. "Once you arrive there," the attendants said, "you will be provided with vouchers for a hotel and meals, and then you will leave the following morning for Durango."

The reality in Albuquerque was not quite what we envisioned: We had a difficult time finding someone from the airline to help us, and when we did, it took about two hours before we finally got our vouchers and a hotel name and address. The shuttle dropped us off and left, but when we walked into the hotel, the man at the front desk laughed and said that there was no possible way the airline would have given us a reservation, because they were totally booked. "In fact, all hotels in town are booked," he said. "There is a convention in town, and there are no rooms available anywhere." We could not believe the airline would have been so irresponsible as to send us to a hotel without a reservation, but we painfully realized that it had been the only way for them to get rid of us at the airport.

We argued, we waited, we begged ... but to no avail. The hotel simply had no rooms. Finally, someone came who made a few phone calls and gave us the name of a hotel and address where we could stay. "It's about half an hour from here by taxi," he said, "but you will be able to sleep there." That was music to our ears, as it was around 10 p.m. by then.

We flagged a taxi, got our belongings in it, and told the driver where we were headed. As he started driving without saying a word, I couldn't help but notice how immense he was: He was driving an old Lincoln Continental, a comfortably wide car, and yet his shoulders spread from the driver's window fully halfway across the interior of the car. *Big!* I thought. *And probably very strong. I hope he is safe.* I did not feel safe.

At one point, our driver told us to close our windows and lock the doors. He instructed us not to pay attention to anyone if he had to stop at a streetlight. Ana and I looked at each other, sharing our concern. The driver then proceeded to question why we would want to go to the hotel we had told him about. "Who recommended *that* hotel?" he said. "It is not safe in that area. I suggest you lock your door when you get to your room, and don't open it for anyone at anytime until you are ready to leave tomorrow morning." My wife didn't like what she heard, and we started reconsidering our options. We asked him if the Albuquerque airport was open all night, and he said yes. So we asked him to turn around at once and take us back to the airport. We would not sleep much, but at least we would feel safer.

I couldn't help feeling a bit like Joseph in Bethlehem when he was unable to find a room for his pregnant wife, Mary. It must have been horrible for him not to be able to provide a shelter or a decent roof. He had no reservations, and there was a large event (the census) in town. He knocked on several doors, but everywhere he went he heard the same answer. Of course, my wife was not about to give birth to the Son of God, but I was really tense, almost desperate. I felt completely useless and unable to provide my family with a safe place to sleep. And I was extremely mad at the airline for having lied to us so blatantly.

As we were nearing the airport, the driver said, "Look, there seems to be room at that Motel 6!" He pulled off the highway, talked to the man at the front desk, and then informed us that there was one smoking room available. We took it, thanked our angel driver, and crashed on our beds.

(In doing some fact-checking with my daughter, she said that she remembered the episode clearly: "The taxi driver had a huge back—when he got out to get our luggage, I couldn't believe how broad his shoulders were. The hotel room stank; it was a smoking room. We went to sleep past midnight and had to get up at 4:30 a.m. They should have let us stay at the airport to begin with..." It is amazing what an eight-year-old can remember ten years later!) Anyway, everything went well after that. We even got an apology in writing from the airline!

That night, I experienced firsthand what it felt like to be a stranger, a foreigner, homeless in a city where danger could be felt waiting around every corner. I remembered clearly how God commands us to make room in our homes for the stranger, and I thanked Him for providing us with an honest and resourceful taxi driver.

Then the King will say to those on his right, "Come, you who are blessed by my Father; take your inheritance, the kingdom prepared for you since the creation of the world. For I was hungry and you gave me something to eat, I was thirsty and you gave me something to drink, I was a stranger and you invited me in, I needed clothes and you clothed me, I was sick and you looked after me, I was in prison and you came to visit me." Then the righteous will answer him, "Lord, when did we see you hungry and feed you, or thirsty and give you something to drink? When did we see you a stranger and invite you in, or needing clothes and clothe you? When did we see you sick or in prison and go to visit you?" The King will reply, "I tell you the truth, whatever you did for one of the least of these brothers of mine, you did for me."

—Matthew 25:34-40

This story would not be complete without honoring my wife, Ana María. In the early 1990s, we were living in Ann Arbor, Michigan, while I attended graduate school at the University of Michigan. Each summer there would be a weeklong event called the Ann Arbor Street Art Fair, a time when so many visitors flooded the city that the population would double. In 1992, Ana was visiting the Art Fair when she came across a group of ten musicians from the Andes in South America. As she listened to their music on the street, she was moved by God to help them. Only a few minutes later, one of the musicians asked her directly if she knew of a place where they could stay, as they couldn't find anything.

When I got home to our two-bedroom apartment that evening, Ana told me that she had invited them to stay with us. "But you don't even know them!" I protested. "And …and …there are too many of them, and they are wandering artists, and they may be dangerous, and we are on a very tight budget, and we really have no room!" I presented my very reasonable arguments in a quick crescendo, but Ana disarmed me with one swift stroke: "I believe that God is asking us to open our home to them. They are strangers in a foreign land."

So we did. We borrowed mattresses from our neighbors and set the musicians up in our small basement. Ana prepared dinner for the whole group, and the three of us spent the night locked in our bedroom. They left after breakfast the following morning, and nothing bad happened. Ana heard God's voice and chose to obey. May we all be attentive to the Word of God.

I was a stranger, and you invited me in…

TAXI DRIVERS

YOU MEET THEM everywhere; they are an essential part of your trip. They come from India, from Colombia, from Afghanistan—sometimes you feel they must be coming from anywhere but the country you are visiting. There are quiet ones and gregarious ones. There are invasive ones who make you feel uncomfortable because you remember some rules of personal safety that you were taught by your company, such as "do not provide information about who you are or how long you are traveling" and "make sure the taxi driver knows that you and someone else knows who's driving you."

There are different types of taxi drivers in different places, but all over the world you find "informal taxi drivers." These are the ones who have no license to provide their services. They belong to no formal company, and they can range anywhere from being slightly dishonest to outright dangerous.

In 1998, I was giving a presentation at a medical conference before the Central American and Caribbean Games in Maracaibo, Venezuela. My flight had arrived at the Maiquetía airport too late for a same-day connection to Maracaibo, so I had decided to stay overnight at a hotel close to the airport. As I was picking up my luggage, I ran into Dr. Francisco Arroyo and his wife, and we talked about riding together to the hotel. A taxi driver approached us and offered his services and, in our distraction, we did not realize that he was an "informal driver" until he pulled up in his car. Francisco and I looked at each other, but neither one of us was smart enough to reject the service. We later regretted the decision when the driver started driving us through dark and narrow streets. We were so apprehensive that when he inquired as to whether our company was paying for the hotel, we both asked why he wanted to know and demanded that we be driven directly to the hotel we had chosen. The driver claimed that he was trying to save us money (he should have charged us a reasonable fare instead), but we never bought his story. Luckily, Francisco and I can talk and laugh about it now.

In Argentina, you have your regular taxicab, or you can get a *remise* (pronounced "re-miss"). *Remiseros* tend to be well-educated people who have lost their jobs and need to make a living driving. They own a nice-looking car, operate under license, and are preferred as a means of city transportation for business people. Back in 1999, my wife, Ana María, and I were visiting Argentina while doing a series of presentations on behalf of the Gatorade® Sport Science Institute and Roche Pharmaceutical. Our driver while we were in Buenos Aires was a *remisero* named Manolo. When we first met him, I told him that I had been in Argentina twice and mentioned that "fortunately, this time I was able to come with my wife." He misunderstood me (I guess he was used to travelers who would rather be "free" by themselves) and started explaining what a privilege it should be for me to be with her. Ana quickly agreed and reassured him that we were delighted to be together.

Manolo was surprised at the kind, gentle, and respectful way that we talked to him. He drove us around several times. When we parted, we felt as if we were leaving a friend behind. His story was sad: His wife had a brain tumor, they were separated, and he had lost his full-time driver job with Roche due to restructuring. Now, he was forced to drive as a *remisero*. We shared our faith with him, encouraged him, and gave him hope.

One year later, during my next trip to Argentina, Ana sent Manolo a Christian music CD and a Bible. I spoke with him on the phone and made sure that he had received the gift. In return, sometime later he gave us two small mementos that expressed his gratitude for remembering him. We had been instruments in God's hands.

TAXI DRIVERS

Seven years later, I was in London. A young man, Barty Dearden, was driving me around during the shoot for a Gatorade commercial. He gave me another opportunity to share my faith ...but that is another story.

Always be prepared to give an answer to everyone who asks you to give the reason for the hope that you have. But do this with gentleness and respect.
—1 Peter 3:15-16

COMPUTER CRISIS

HAVE YOU EVER noticed how some laptop manufacturers prey on your fears of having an accident that will make you lose all the data on your computer? They know what they're doing. If you have never had such an experience, I hope you never do. It is not until it happens that you realize how limited your backups are.

I got my first laptop computer toward the end of 1997, when I started consulting for the Gatorade® Sports Science Institute. It was thick, it was white, and it was heavy, but it was portable and more powerful than my four-year-old desktop. That laptop traveled with me a few hundred thousand miles without any falls or coffee spills, and only two electric mishaps. Then the time came to replace it in May 2000, even though it had survived the millennium bug.

My new laptop was ready. All my data had been transferred, and the old computer had been disposed of. During one of my brief visits to company headquarters, I asked the tech support person to install two programs to enable me to communicate with the company. Later, I was sitting in an important meeting when she opened the door, walked in, and whispered in my ear, "Luis, you keep good backups, right? Well, that's good." Then she left. I am not kidding.

Now, as an independent consultant, I worked on my own. Yes, I kept regular backups of most of my files, but I was not aware that I was non-systematic about it. I could not stay in the meeting for long; I had to find out why the tech person had asked such a strange question at such an odd time. The answer was simple: My computer had crashed several times, and the tech support person had decided to reformat the hard drive and reinstall the operating system and all the rest of the software. She didn't think twice about it, because all the computers in the building were backed up automatically every day. Then she realized that I was a visitor!

Suddenly, all my files were potentially lost—doctoral dissertation, research data, lectures—years and years of work. Even worse, I was traveling. It would be another four days before I could get back home to check what had survived. I was in shock and had no idea what to do. So I picked up the phone and called my wife, Ana María, for emotional support. I was not ready for what followed.

"Oh, I am so glad you called, this is terrible," she said. "She's got syphilis. No wonder she didn't want to go to the doctor!" An entire book could not explain the meaning of that sentence to us, but two paragraphs will have to do.

After our first daughter, Ana Victoria, was born, Ana María had two miscarriages, a few health challenges and a surgery, after which we simply could not have more children. Six years later, we started praying about adoption and decided to go ahead. Over the course of two years we took all the necessary steps, prepared our home and our hearts, learned about our limitations, and ran into all the deficiencies of the Costa Rican adoption process.

Then the day came: A thirty-year-old single woman was three months pregnant and simply could not keep her baby. We had some interviews, started supporting her, and made sure she could get proper medical care. Well, that was the problem: she skipped the appointments because she knew from the very start that she had syphilis. Ana and I knew that we were not prepared to raise a baby who might be born blind or seriously handicapped in some way. We felt guilty and struggled with feelings of selfishness, but, after praying and talking about it many times, we knew that we did not have the emotional strength to do it.

I hung up the phone, walked out of the building, and cried in despair. I could not even embrace Ana, who was in much greater pain than me! What a horrible moment to be away from home! Where should I go? What should I do? Pastor and mentor Robert Sabean says that one of the riches of memorizing Scriptures is that you can recite them in times of difficulty, no matter where you are. So I began to pray: "*Sólo en Dios encuentro paz, mi salvación viene de Él. Sólo Dios me salva y me protege. No caeré, porque Él es mi refugio*" (Psalm 62:1-2). "*Todo mi ser se consume, pero Dios es mi herencia eterna, y el que sostiene mi corazón*" (Psalm 73:26). Over and over, I prayed to God in my pain. He chose to let me experience that pain for a long time. I felt that it was too long.

After considerable stress and uncertainty, the computer crisis was eventually solved, with the result that I lost only two weeks of work. The family issue took two more years, during which time I would regularly pray Psalm 42–43 from the bottom of my heart. The baby, praise God, was adopted by two friends of ours whom God had prepared for that particular moment.

> *Deep calls to deep in the roar of your waterfalls; all your waves and breakers have swept over me.*
> —Psalm 42:7

EVANGELISTIC ZEAL

I OFTEN WONDER to what extent sharing the gospel with others is a matter of obedience to God's Word and to what extent it has to do with one's personality. The fact is, I have a hard time evangelizing the passenger next to me. Preaching the gospel to a total stranger is simply not my style. Yet I cannot help but feel that I should be doing something about it.

For that reason, I admire people like my brother David Mijares. David (pronounced "Dah-vid") lived in Costa Rica for a few years, working for a Christian campus ministry as a Catholic missionary. Within a few weeks, everyone who rode the bus to the university knew that he was "some sort of a priest," as he would regularly talk about God to whoever dared to sit next to him. He would not waste any time. Ever.

Back in the late 1980s, David was waiting at the airport in El Salvador. He was trying to make the best use of his layover time at the gate, so he started a conversation with the man next to him with the sole intention of sharing the good news.

"I am an engineer by training," he said, "but I now work as a missionary, devoting 100 percent of my time to preaching the gospel to university students. There is nothing better in life than knowing Jesus and working for Him."

"I can understand what you mean," the man replied, "as that is also what I do for a living."

"Oh, really?" said David. "What do you do?"

"I am the Bishop of San Salvador," the man replied.

This bishop must have been delighted to meet such a zealous young man. To me, that was just like David!

In the presence of God and of Christ Jesus, who will judge the living and the dead, and in view of his appearing and his kingdom, I give you this charge: Preach the Word; be prepared in season and out of season; correct, rebuke and encourage—with great patience and careful instruction.
—2 Timothy 4:1-2

MY GREATEST FEAR

W E ALL HAVE fears. Some are greater, some are smaller, and some are more real than others. As a child, I was terrified of the man in the closet—a man who was not there. Years later, I was afraid of forgetting about any particular college test and showing up unprepared—again, something not very realistic. Only a week ago, I had a nightmare where the Devil was pulling down my bed sheets from both sides, and I could not move or speak. I am sure that I screamed "UUUUUY!" right as I woke up in my hotel room, drenched in sweat. Good thing my wife was safe at home. I would have really scared her.

However, my greatest fear has always been to suffocate underwater. Funny thing that I would choose to learn scuba diving and be trained as a lifeguard! The fear is real: I can dive, swim underwater, hold my breath, and even practice leaving my scuba tanks in the deep end to swim underwater the length of a twenty-five-yard pool, slowly blowing out all the air in my lungs. But the moment there is an obstacle between the surface and me, I panic. I cannot tolerate the possibility of not being able to resurface.

In December 2000, I was in Cooranbong, Australia. I had just had a really good time collaborating with Darren Morton, an exercise scientist from Avondale College. We had been working regularly on our research project, but we had also shared a few outdoor adventures. He and his brother took me on a hike by the ocean. The scenery was awesome, although it was not a hike for the faint of heart. At one point we came to a cliff and had to jump into the crashing waves some four or five meters below. Darren's brother jumped to show me the timing, and I jumped next. No problem. We swam a couple hundred yards and came to a bay where we started treading water. Everything was okay until they told me that the only way out was to swim underwater through a five-meter-long tunnel to reach a cave. How in the world had they discovered this place? It didn't matter. All that mattered at that point was the fact that I was not going in.

Darren went in, and his brother followed. A few minutes later, Darren came out again, finding me frozen and unable to go under. He tried to convince me, only to witness for thirty long minutes my inability to overcome this fear. The waves crashing on the rocks around us were probably more dangerous, but it didn't matter. I simply couldn't swim into the cave. I had a wife and daughter. I couldn't die.

Finally, I prayed to God for courage and protection and went in. It was all worth it. The cave was amazing: tall, with a bit of light coming through the opposite end, showing us the exit. I had conquered my fear …if only for a brief moment.

I tell you, my friends, do not be afraid of those who kill the body and after that can do no more. But I will show you whom you should fear: Fear him who, after the killing of the body, has power to throw you into hell. Yes, I tell you, fear him. Are not five sparrows sold for two pennies? Yet not one of them is forgotten by God. Indeed, the very hairs of your head are all numbered. Don't be afraid; you are worth more than many sparrows.
—Luke 12:4-7

LACK OF CONTROL

M Y FIRST BUSINESS trip took place in September 1997. I flew with my boss to Argentina, and it was a great experience. He showed me the ropes: I learned there were such things as Admiral Clubs and upgrades and that it might be smarter, albeit expensive, to eat at the airport as I waited for the boarding time. After a few interesting experiences, I asked a naïve question: "Bob, have you ever been stranded, say, in Australia, or had your flight cancelled or something like that? What in the world do you do?"

Bob smiled, watching me make the gestures of an intense Latino who was distraught at the mere possibility of such a thing. He responded in his cool, Bob-Murray style: "Nothing. Yes, it has happened to me, but I simply adjust and do nothing. What could I do, anyway? I know I have no control under those circumstances." Those were perhaps the most important words of wisdom I received during the whole trip.

Five years later, I was visiting Buenos Aires once again. I had to deliver several presentations that were not finished, but I was arriving twenty-four hours early and had plenty of time to rest and complete my assignments. Resting is important for me after an all-night flight, because even though I usually sleep well during such flights, it is for only five hours or so. I need my seven hours of sleep per night.

As usual, I was fast asleep when the crew got restless, about one hour before landing, with their breakfast and cleanup routine. We approached the Buenos Aires airport on time, around eight a.m. Then I heard the ominous voice of the captain over the PA system announcing that the plane could not land because of strong crosswinds at the airport, or something to that effect. (As usual, the PA system was too loud and the sound quality too poor, and that's all I could understand. The captain must have excelled in Garble Language 101—that class that all airline pilots take when physicians are taking Advanced Prescription Writing.) We circled for almost an hour before being diverted to Paraguay.

In Paraguay, of course, we were not allowed to disembark. We stayed inside the plane for a couple of hours while the aircraft was refueled and the captain kept in touch with Buenos Aires. Needless to say, for most of that time we were asked to stay in our seats, and we could not use the bathrooms. My laptop battery was totally spent, and my personal batteries were draining quickly. My tension had started building up after we left Buenos Aires. How long was this going to take? Were they telling me the truth? How was I going to get my presentations finished? The first question was, of course, the most important one and the most difficult to answer. This was lack of control at its best.

Finally, we took off. The captain said that we would make another attempt to land in Buenos Aires. When that didn't work, the plane turned around and headed for Montevideo, Uruguay, which was only a few miles away. We landed there and were allowed to get off the plane. As a special treatment to compensate for our troubles, the two-hundred-and-some passengers were allowed to enter the VIP lounge to await further news. The lounge was so crowded that it would have been much more comfortable to wait outside in the general gate area, but we were all too tired to realize it.

I plugged in my computer and tried to work on my presentations, but I was constantly interrupted by rumors such as "they are going to hire a boat to ship us over to Buenos Aires," or "the winds are so strong no boats are allowed on Rio de la Plata," or "apparently ours was the only plane that could not land in Ezeiza today." After waiting about six hours with no information at all from the airline—shifting from trying to work on my computer to standing in line for the bathroom to climbing the walls of the Montevideo airport—we were called back to the gate. We boarded, took off, landed, and the nightmare was over. My partners picked me up and drove me to the hotel, just the way it should have been, only twelve hours and about ten thousand kilocalories of emotional energy later. I wonder why the airline magazines don't have a section for travelers to tell similar stories…

Despite experiences like this one, I try to remind myself that not having control at all times may be healthy, because it allows more room for God to intervene, to show His love for us, and to pour His grace on us. Too bad that losing control still represents such a challenge to me!

In his heart a man plans his course, but the LORD determines his steps.
—Proverbs 16:9

GUILTY?

I N LATE AUGUST 2002, I landed in Lima, Peru, after a short three-hour flight from Costa Rica. I was supposed to help with testing a local triathlete, and I had brought a device with me to measure environmental heat stress. The man checking my luggage in customs wanted to know what it was and how much I had paid for it. I explained that I was a scientist and that the device was simply an environmental thermometer capable of measuring relative humidity and radiation heat. I told him that it was used; I must have paid 500,000 Colones for it a few years back. He wanted to know how much that was in local currency, and because I did not know the exchange rate, he lost his patience and sent me to a special window where I had to fill out some paperwork and pay taxes.

I grudgingly took my luggage to the window and asked a woman for help. "*El encargado* [the man in charge] is not here," she said. "He will be back in a few minutes." After a "few" minutes turned into ten minutes and then fifteen minutes, I started getting impatient. I knew that impatience is a terrible companion in that type of situation, so I kept myself busy by watching all the people going through customs. A woman with a bag so heavy she could hardly drag it. A man with two beautiful German Shepherd dogs. A tired family. After a little while, I realized that nobody was watching *me*.

What would prevent me from leaving? I thought. *Do I have my passport and other documents? Yes. Do I have the WBGT thermometer? Yes. My suitcase? Yes. Portable computer? Everything is with me. Okay. Breathe. If I simply started walking toward the exit, who would stop me? Okay, I am already beyond the customs booths. I've already cleared immigration. Okay, okay. What if somebody questions me? I can always claim that I am looking for El Encargado. Great, I have a plan. After all, I have been waiting for thirty minutes now and nobody is helping me! I'm out of here.*

My heart racing, but otherwise looking absolutely calm, I headed for the exit. I crossed the doors, found a driver holding up my name, and I was gone. *That was easy! I am so clever! And to think that I could have been there still waiting to pay some taxes that I shouldn't even have to pay…*

The testing went well, we got some media coverage, and the whole mission was a success. Two days later, I went back to the airport to catch a direct flight back home. I checked in, got my boarding pass, cleared security, and gave my passport to the immigration official. She stamped it, gave it back, and sent me off to my gate. Then I heard her calling after me.

"Sir, excuse me! Would you come back for a moment, please? May I have your passport?" She kept me there for a minute, and then a police officer showed up. He took my passport and asked me to accompany him. We both walked in silence to a small room, where he ordered me to wait and then locked the door. Up to that moment, I had not remembered *anything* about the incident I had had with customs when I arrived, but now it all came back to me instantly. I suddenly felt as if I were standing naked in front of my boss. How did they notice? Did they catch me on video? What would I say now? Certainly, I had not contemplated this! And I was going to miss my flight, too.

What a difference it makes to have a clean conscience! At that moment, I did not. When the policeman returned half an hour later, I was a nervous wreck. But he didn't notice; he simply apologized. He told me that they had someone with a similar name on a blacklist and said that it had all been a mistake. He encouraged me to hurry and catch my flight, and I didn't think twice about it. Four hours later, I was landing in Costa Rica. In this case, I did not have to pay for my crime because I was not caught. When I stand in front of the Lord, I will not have to pay for my crimes because He was wounded for my transgressions and bruised for my iniquities (see Isaiah 53:5).

> *Once you were alienated from God and were enemies in your minds because of your evil behavior. But now he has reconciled you by Christ's physical body through death to present you holy in his sight, without blemish and free from accusation—if you continue in your faith, established and firm, not moved from the hope held out in the gospel. This is the gospel that you heard and that has been proclaimed to every creature under heaven, and of which I, Paul, have become a servant.*
>
> —Colossians 1:21-23

WHERE IS MY SUITCASE?

HAVE YOU EVER wondered why people chase their luggage when it's coming off the carousel as if they would never see it again instead of waiting for it to come around a second time? Well, in Costa Rica, there is a very good reason. Experienced travelers know that there are two men responsible for pulling all the luggage off the carousel as soon as possible. They take the bags and pile them in a corner, where they are not easily found. The procedure must be a leftover from decades ago when there were no carousels. As a result, at least half of the tourists can be found waiting patiently for their bags until no more come out, and then someone points them to the corner where they wade through the mess and get their things. You would think that after a few years of this someone would have figured it out and sent those two men someplace else. But this presupposes that someone is actually managing the system.

Anyway, almost everywhere I go it is the same thing: even the most kind, elderly woman will push and shove to get her suitcase off the carousel immediately. Maybe she wants to rescue it as soon as possible from the handle-breaking, strap-eating, buckle-grinding machine. In my case, I want to make sure that nobody else takes it.

The fact is, we all get a bit anxious when waiting for our bags. This is particularly true when arriving at a place such as Chicago O'Hare at 1 a.m. on a cold winter night, and your jacket is in the suitcase. Or when you've had to put something valuable—an important gift, a tailor-made

31

suit, a piece of scientific equipment—in your checked luggage. At that point, your attention focuses on that single thing; that familiar suitcase with your name on it.

I place most of the blame for my anxiety on how the airlines handle things. When everything works well, it's fine. But the system does not seem to contemplate the possibility of errors, and errors abound. That's when I suffer. I traveled to Brazil a few years ago, and my suitcase did not arrive with me. When I followed up with the airline two days later, they told me that the suitcase had arrived but they had not delivered it to me because I was not in my hotel room when they called. I wonder how many people travel to another country just to sit around in their hotel room?

You would expect that if you were flying business class or first class—even if only because of an upgrade—your luggage would receive preferential treatment. Not so. Everything else being equal, I would choose to fly the airline that handled luggage better. If you are reading this and you are in the airline business, there's a tip for you.

What amazes me is how people can become attached to so little—just fifty pounds of stuff. By contrast, in Matthew 10:9-10, when Jesus sent His disciples out on a mission He told them to go forth without spare clothes or anything. They surely avoided many upsets. I guess their lives were a bit simpler, too.

And why do you worry about clothes? See how the lilies of the field grow. They do not labor or spin. Yet I tell you that not even Solomon in all his splendor was dressed like one of these. If that is how God clothes the grass of the field, which is here today and tomorrow is thrown into the fire, will he not much more clothe you, O you of little faith?
—Matthew 6:28-30

TRUST

O N MY FIRST trip to the University of Loughborough in the United Kingdom during Easter week of 2003, I almost got into trouble for not carrying enough cash with me. I had been advised to hire a limo service to take me from Heathrow Airport to the university, a two-and-a-half-hour trip. On my way there, I found out that the driver could not process a credit card for payment. I got a little nervous, but the driver assured me that we should be able to exchange some traveler's checks at the hotel.

Not so. "No problem," the driver said. "When are you leaving? Will you need a ride to the Birmingham airport? I'd be happy to take you there, and you can pay me then." Did I get that right? A trusting taxi driver? I was grateful he would trust me that way, which I think is something quite extraordinary these days. I owed him the equivalent of $190.

When the driver picked me up three days later, he drove me to the airport and showed me where to get cash. At that point, I would not have been offended if he had kept my suitcase until I returned, as the bill now amounted to $250. But, to my surprise, he unloaded everything and told me he would be waiting for me. I didn't even consider the possibility of not coming back. Well, my heart did not. My flesh, on the other hand, jumped up and said, *What prevents you from going straight to the boarding gate?*

33

"I would never do that!" I said back.

That's precisely the point; your life is sooo boring. Do something exciting for a change!

"It doesn't even make sense. I wouldn't be saving any money; my company is paying for the expense anyway."

But he deserves it. Show him you are smarter than him.

You may have engaged in a similar argument with the Devil at least once in your life. *Never* a good idea.

I will never know why this British taxi driver chose to trust me, a total stranger from Latin America. Is it possible that he was a Christian, a man who listened attentively to God, and that he was told to help me out? He chose to obey. So did I, by the grace of God. I trust that we will someday meet in heaven and enjoy remembering this story.

Be self-controlled and alert. Your enemy the devil prowls around like a roaring lion looking for someone to devour. Resist him, standing firm in the faith, because you know that your brothers throughout the world are undergoing the same kind of sufferings.

—1 Peter 5:8-9

WHEN WE REFUSE TO THINK

WHEN WE REFUSE to be rational, bad things can happen to our spiritual life. I experienced this firsthand a few years ago. I do not intend to excuse my behavior and blame it on something else, but I must have undergone what Dr. James Dobson calls a "testosterone shower." I am a pretty rational person, but my actions in this instance did not make sense at all.

It was the kind of thing that can happen easily to you if you are a frequent traveler. The pattern goes something like this: your flight is delayed or cancelled, or your hotel reservation is not honored, or you have recently experienced some frustrations at home with your wife or husband. Whatever the circumstances, the result is the same: you strongly feel that you are not getting what you deserve. Then, out of nowhere, someone shows you a special kindness, maybe even a basic courtesy. But instead of quietly thanking God for it, your imagination—or your actions—pick it up and run with it.

This happened to me one time in Mexico City when, after a presentation on hydration for athletic performance during a conference, a tall, slim marathon runner and her two friends came up to me and said, "Doctor, your presentation was so clear and interesting. You are our hero!" Such a simple statement, and yet her words reverberated in my mind and her image distracted me for the rest of that trip.

35

The same was true with NoNami. I met NoNami during an exhausting tour in Brazil during April and May 2001. She was one of many nutrition students attending my presentation, and one of a few to come up to me afterward to discuss a few topics. Nothing in particular happened, besides the naturally rewarding academic discussion with a young and enthusiastic individual. Okay, I admit that I noticed she was very beautiful. That was it.

In November of that same year, I was invited to return to São Paulo for a nutrition conference. It was an amazing event, with some seven hundred participants in attendance, of which at most a dozen were male. I went up to the podium during a break to prepare for my presentation and, as I was setting up, one particular face in the front row stood out. It was NoNami. I came down to say hello, exchanged a few sentences, and returned to the podium to deliver my lecture.

We made eye contact too many times. After I finished, she came up to me to congratulate me, and we spent a good hour visiting posters and talking. The fact that she spoke little Spanish or English, and I very little Portuguese, did not seem to matter. My emotions were totally upside down. I was captivated by her beautiful smile and her attentiveness. Fortunately, she had to stand by her poster and talk to others, and I was distracted by other people and my responsibilities. My plane left that evening, but I left my heart in São Paulo.

What do I mean, *I left my heart in São Paulo?* What was I thinking? Well, I wasn't. That is precisely the mystery of the male heart. Others may attempt to pass a trailer truck on a moped at night on a narrow mountain road. The end result could be the same.

Back home, I reflected on the whole situation. Here I was, a Christian and a married man. I was at least twice her age. I would never leave my family to go in pursuit of some woman in Brazil. I did not even know if NoNami was attracted to me; she may have just been showing some basic Brazilian hospitality to a visiting professor and nothing more. I knew that the first thing to do was to *not* find out, because my heart was extremely vulnerable at that moment. So I destroyed her business card and deleted a couple of old e-mails in which we had discussed some scientific question or other. I had no way of getting back in touch with her. I shared my experience with my closer brothers from my church and made a commitment with them to be open about this temptation.

Why make such a big deal about it? For one thing, Jesus has told us, "You have heard that it was said, 'Do not commit adultery.' But I tell you that anyone who looks at a woman lustfully has already committed adultery with her in his heart" (Matthew 5:27-28). In addition, I knew that this could result in greater trouble in the future. As C. S. Lewis wrote, "Good and evil both increase at compound interest. That is why the little decisions you and I make every day are of such infinite importance. The smallest good act today is the capture of a strategic point from which, a few months later, you may be able to go on to victories you never dreamed of. An apparently trivial indulgence in lust or anger today is the loss of a ridge or railway line or bridgehead from which the enemy may launch an attack otherwise impossible."[1]

Fast-forward to August 2003. I am back in São Paulo and, honestly, I don't even remember NoNami. I have not heard from her since I saw her almost two years earlier. I am in Brazil to cohost a sports nutrition conference and am participating as a speaker and moderator of two roundtable discussions. I am well prepared; I helped to choose all the speakers for the program. But, in a last-minute change, my local colleagues decided to replace a nutritionist in my roundtable discussion. The new member is NoNami—and the enemy launches the attack without hesitation from the ridge I had surrendered so long ago.

All I remember is a storm of emotions turning me upside down. Just like a teenager, I wanted to sit by her in the audience and during dinner, and I couldn't keep my eyes off of her. Those were two very long days as I struggled not to do anything stupid like talk to her about how I was feeling or anything else of a personal nature. *Thinking stupid* was bad enough.

The late-night flight back home was a long one, too, as I could not fall asleep. Every time I heard a love song in my earphones, it struck the wrong chords in my heart and gave wings to my imagination. I was going back home victorious, but wounded.

Hurry! Hurry back home! Go back to Ana! Guard your eyes and your heart! Conquer that ridge, and never give it up again!

And the next time, please, don't refuse to think.

Drink water from your own cistern, running water from your own well. Should your springs overflow in the streets, your streams of water in the public squares? Let them be yours alone, never to be shared with strangers. May your fountain be blessed, and may you rejoice in the wife of your youth. A loving doe, a graceful deer—may her breasts satisfy you always, may you ever be captivated by her love.

—Proverbs 5:15-19

BE STILL

I T IS MADDENING. That dead time around takeoff and landing, only five to ten minutes long (although I have experienced it to be an hour or longer), makes you crazy because you cannot watch TV or use your cell phone or your computer during that time. The pilot and flight attendants also make sure that you cannot use this dead time to sleep or even read, giving you crucial announcements such as "today we will be flying at 32,000 feet" or "we give a special welcome to those of you who are members of our MirageMiles program." If you are lucky enough, all the announcements will be given in two or three languages.

Invariably, as you sit there just waiting, you will feel the urge to use the bathroom. You will realize you forgot to get something out of your bag sitting in the overhead bin. You will feel you must recline the back of your seat at once, even if you then forget about it for the rest of your flight. Why is this dead time so difficult?

One reason that comes to my mind is because we simply are not used to being still. When we don't have something to distract us or keep us busy, we have to face ourselves. This is healthy to do every now and then; in fact, God Himself has told us, "Be still, and know that I am God" (Psalm 46:10). So until we build up our ability to be still, why not put this time to good use by talking to God?

I am definitely not the type of person who can isolate himself in such an environment and listen attentively to God. But I can recite memorized Bible verses. And I can intercede, recalling special needs and placing them before the Lord.

Teach us to number our days aright, that we may gain a heart of wisdom.

—Psalm 90:12

A FRUSTRATED
ATHLETE

I AM NOT naturally gifted to be an outstanding athlete, but I have discipline and I enjoy exercise. I love training regularly with a clear goal in mind. Interestingly, every single time I have felt that I was in top condition, something has happened to bring me down to earth (and a bit lower). Every time that I have felt I was reaching the level of fitness I wanted, I would get hit by a cold that would beat me for ten days and leave me weak and flabby, or I would pull a muscle, or I would injure myself in some other stupid way. It happened when I was younger, and it keeps happening to this day. And my body detrains *so* quickly…

This is particularly frustrating when it occurs right before the event or competition that motivated my training. One time, my friend Otto invited me to join him and some friends on the Arenal Tour, a two-day recreational bike ride around Lake Arenal. I had been trying to recover from a back injury, so I had not been riding my mountain bike regularly. Because of many time restrictions, I started pedaling regularly two months before the event—three times each week on a stationary bike at home (the discipline part) and outdoors on Sundays (the fun part). By the end of January, I felt that I was ready to do the tour and even pedal up the Arenal Volcano in a single day. Then, four days before the trip, I fell sick with the all-too-common cold.

In the same way, every time I think I have my act together—every time I feel free from sin—I stumble and fall flat on my face. I can hear

41

Paul's words: "So, if you think you are standing firm, be careful that you don't fall!" (1 Corinthians 10:12).

What does this have to do with business travel? Not much, really …unless you realize you could fall flat on your face during a trip while thinking you were standing firm!

> *It is for freedom that Christ has set us free. Stand firm, then, and do not let yourselves be burdened again by a yoke of slavery.*
>
> —Galatians 5:1

WHO AM I?

I CAN SOMETIMES relate to Jackie Chan's character in the action movie *Who Am I?* I often have my own version of an identity crisis. Going through the U.S. immigration booths at least a hundred times and being fingerprinted and photographed at least sixty can make a person start to wonder who he or she really is. My passport reads with absolute clarity "Número de Pasaporte/Passport No. 1-2345-6789," but try to use that number on your I-94 form and you'll get, "No, sir, that is not your passport number. You must write down L987654 [the sequence number]."

Finally, after being forced to go back to the end of the line a couple of times, I decided to let go of the number I was born with—the number that fulfills *all* official transactions and procedures in Costa Rica (and most other countries in the world)—and please the U.S. immigration officers. After all, I have at least a dozen different identities for computing purposes, each one of which to please the peculiar requirements of my employer, my Internet service provider, my music club, my electronic newspaper…

As a result of "Googling" myself a few months ago, I realized that there is more than one Luis Fernando Aragon in the world. (Hey, that's *my* name! Didn't my parents secure worldwide copyright for it?) I was also told by an immigration officer this past May that "apparently, many people with a name as common as yours are wanted by international police, so you will need to accompany an officer to a room for inter-rogation." *Their* interrogation, that is, because my only question (how come this has never happened before, given the fact that I cross U.S. borders at least a dozen times a year?) was not answered, and I wisely chose not to push it. This limited my detention time to thirty minutes.

In all the countries I visit in Europe and the Americas, I have to use the longer, slower lines for the non-nationals (in the U.S., I am called an "alien," just like E.T.). Sadly enough, in my own country I have to use the longer lines for the citizens (we come after tourists in my country's priorities). Because of typos, my name is different in different hotel chains—having two "last names" also doesn't help. My older passport expiration date read 09/10/05, in the format YY/MM/DD (showing first the year in two digits, then the month, then the day), but apparently no other country in the world uses this logic, which for several years caused its share of aggravation whenever I tried to explain that the passport was still valid. Fortunately, my birth date appeared in the same format and, of course, there are not fifty-eight days in a month or fifty-eight months in a year, allowing me to prove that the first two digits represented the year.

All of these seemingly small details start to undermine my identity as a son of God. I am just another person, another passenger, another hotel guest, another tired traveler, another nobody. I become anonymous. This anonymity causes two problems. First, I don't get what I think I deserve—I don't get the respect and love I get from my family, neighbors, or close co-workers. Second, I am tempted to do things that I would never do where people actually know me. I know that some temptations are easy to overcome when you are surrounded by friends or family in a public setting, but that they get stronger when you are in private, such as when you are in a foreign country in the absence of a "what would people think if they found out" environment. (It is no secret that this is one characteristic that makes pornography such a difficult challenge for the modern man.)

Losing my identity during travel is, clearly, not a good thing. I find it important to constantly remind myself, *Who am I? I am Ana's husband. I am the father of Esteban and Ana Victoria. I am a Christian who loves*

God and wants to be obedient, regardless of the situation. I am a forgiven man, a son of God, by the power of the blood of Jesus! The apostle John has stated it clearly:

> *Yet to all who received him, to those who believed in his name, he gave the right to become children of God—children born not of natural descent, nor of human decision or a husband's will, but born of God.*
>
> —John 1:12-13

> *How great is the love the Father has lavished on us, that we should be called children of God! And that is what we are! The reason the world does not know us is that it did not know him. Dear friends, now we are children of God, and what we will be has not yet been made known. But we know that when he appears, we shall be like him, for we shall see him as he is.*
>
> —1 John 3:1-2

Therefore, whether we are at home or in a hotel room, with friends or in the midst of a crowd in the city, acknowledged or disregarded, honored or despised, cared for or ignored, upgraded or cancelled, quiet or tempted, strong or tired, or firm or lonely, let us always keep in mind that above all we are sons and daughters of God. We have dignity and hope that cannot be robbed by failure, or fame, or beauty, or pain, or death, or life, or angels, or powers, or principalities. Nothing can separate us from God's love (see Romans 8:35-39).

JOURNEY 16

SICK ON THE ROAD

B EING SICK AT home is bad enough, but when you are traveling, it really makes for a tough trip. You are tired, in a bad mood, and functioning at only 50 percent of your capacity. And I am not even talking about being *really* sick—just down and out with the common cold. Having a cold while traveling makes you finally understand why babies cry so loud when the plane is landing. (If only the decongestant had worked sooner!)

You make several trips to the pharmacy, looking for that elusive magic potion. Suddenly, your life is clearly focused on a handful of basic goals: breathing, keeping your voice until the end of your presentation, holding your cough and your sneezing while others make their presentations, staying awake during the day, and getting enough sleep at night. You rearrange your agenda, make sure there is enough humidity in your hotel room, and make sure you carry enough tissues in your pocket.

In a way, it is good for us to focus on a few things—even if that involves focusing on things that will get us through a cold. If only we focused the same way on what the Lord has told us, everything else would more readily fall in its place!

But seek first his kingdom and his righteousness, and all these things will be given to you as well.
—Matthew 6:33

47

ON TEMPTATION AND SPORTS TRAINING

W E ALL KNOW pretty well when we are most susceptible to temptation. At least I do. Some trips I start full of energy. I'm optimistic, inspired, and peaceful. (Of course, it helps when I am taking a direct three-hour flight and won't be away for more than three or four days.) Other trips I start under a cloud.

One such trip was back in November 2003. I was scheduled to go to Kusadasi, Turkey, for a European Soccer Coaches conference, where I had committed to giving a presentation on hydration during soccer training and competition. I left home under a cloud. I was tired of all the travel I had been on during the year (fourteen international trips). I knew that it would take me about twenty-eight hours to get there and almost forty to get back home. It was going to be a tough trip.

After a three-hour flight to Miami, a nine-hour flight to London, and then a four-hour flight to Istanbul (each with their respective down times), I had to wait for a few hours to catch my next flight to Izmir. The layover was long, but not long enough for me to go out and tour the city. So I walked around the airport. Then, suddenly, it appeared right before me. I had never, ever imagined that I would face such a temptation, and nothing could have prepared me for it. There, standing taller than me, was a huge stack of Turkish Delight packed in beautifully decorated cans.

Now, I must say that I had never tasted Turkish Delight, but standing there I could sympathize fully with Edmund when he first walked into

Narnia. He was miserable, cold, and angry with his siblings. When he met the White Witch, he believed she was a queen and ate all the Turkish Delight she offered him. I, in turn, was miserable, tired, and willing to accept any apparent kindness or generosity.

And there lies, I believe, one of the great dangers to travelers: When we are tired or frustrated—when the trip has been a disaster—we can easily lower our guard and be tempted even by something as simple and basic as food. What are we to do? Clearly, we have to keep our guard up and resist all temptations. Including Turkish Delight.

Temptation, unlike the discomfort we feel while exercising or training for an athletic event, does not go away easily. When I am breathlessly pedaling uphill—when it feels as if my thighs are burning—I can keep going because I know that I am almost at the top and will then be able to rest. But you never know when temptation will stop. What you do know is that as soon as you yield to it, it will go away—at least momentarily.

James shows us a higher way: "Submit yourselves, then, to God. Resist the devil, and he will flee from you" (James 4:7). When we are tempted, we need to choose that higher way every time, even if we have failed before. Although we can't know for sure what Paul's thorn was in 2 Corinthians 12:8-9, we can say with him, "Three times I pleaded with the Lord to take it away from me. But he said to me, 'My grace is sufficient for you, for my power is made perfect in weakness.' Therefore I will boast all the more gladly about my weaknesses, so that Christ's power may rest on me."

Father, may Your grace be sufficient for me.

No temptation has seized you except what is common to man. And God is faithful; he will not let you be tempted beyond what you can bear. But when you are tempted, he will also provide a way out so that you can stand up under it.

—1 Corinthians 10:13

JOURNEY 18

SPERA NEL SIGNORE

I HAVE SUCH a hard time waiting, especially if I have to wait for hours to board a delayed airplane. On this day, however, I am waiting for John Keating, a dear brother who is arriving on a late flight.

Some background information here is warranted. Not too long ago in Costa Rica, whenever a close relative was flying to another country, that person's family would come to the Juan Santamaría airport to send him or her off. There was a balcony, and people would stand there until the plane took off. A similar ritual would take place upon arrival. Long before 9-11 and heightened security measures, the whole thing died because it simply became impractical. These days when I return from a long trip, nothing would make me happier than having my wife and children waiting for me at the airport, but the thought of them having to wait for an airplane that is arriving two to three hours late convinces me time and time again that it is better to take a taxi.

On this day, my brother's flight was delayed only a bit more than one hour, which was really no big deal. After all, it is good to wait. It's good to exercise regularly in the reality that good things often take time, even if we don't like it. Most often, our prayers are not answered immediately, but we are told to wait for God. Our final, perfect reward will have to wait as well: we wait upon the Lord, putting all of our confidence in Him.

Il Signore e mia luce e mia salvezza, di chi avrò paura?
Il Signore e difesa della mia vita, di chi avrò timore?...
Ascolta, Signore, la mia voce. Io grido: Abbi pietà di me! Rispondimi.
Di te ha detto il mio cuore: "Cercate il suo volto";
Il tuo volto Signore io cercherò. Non nascondermi il tuo volto,
Non respingere con ira il tuo servo.
Solo cerco contemplare la bontà del Signore
Nella terra dei viventi
Spera nel Signore, sii forte
Si rinfranchi il tuo cuore, e spera nel Signore.
Sì, spera nel Signore.

—Psalm 27:1,7-9,13-14,
as recited by Pope John Paul II, Parish of
San Roberto Bellarmino ai Parioli, Rome, March 2, 1980.

The Lord is my light and my salvation—whom shall I fear?
The Lord is the stronghold of my life—of whom shall I be afraid?...
Hear my voice when I call, O Lord;
be merciful to me and answer me.
My heart says of you, "Seek his face!"
Your face, Lord, I will seek.
Do not hide your face from me,
do not turn your servant away in anger ...
I am still confident of this:
I will see the goodness of the Lord in the land of the living.
Wait for the Lord; be strong and take heart and wait for the Lord.

HUNGER

TRAVELING TO SÃO PAULO was certainly an eye opener. I had never seen hunger that way, and I could hardly believe the social contrasts. It's not that they didn't exist in Costa Rica, but I had never experienced them in such a tangible way before. It probably had to do with the fact that Ana María and I were not much into dining—that is, going out to fancy restaurants where you pay more and eat less. But on this trip, the fact that there are *seven to ten million* children living on the streets in Brazil alone, of which I easily saw a few hundred with my own eyes, had a profound impact on me.[1]

Yes, São Paulo is a city full of restaurants. I have been there a dozen times, and my hosts always take me to special places for dinner (and even for lunch). Every time I go, I try to remember how much hunger is being experienced at that very moment. Every time, I try to exercise some self-control, eating little and ordering simple, basic meals. I remind myself that hunger is an everyday reality for too many people.

The issue of hunger took an interesting twist during one business trip to Greece in 2004 for the pre-Olympic conference, a scientific event held every four years in conjunction with the Summer Olympic Games. I woke up in the middle of the night, my mind focused on the idea of how to help food companies be profitable while providing food for poor people. I had often thought about this in the past. I had discussed it with a few business people and even presented the case to a couple of people from PepsiCo®, Gatorade's® parent company, who interviewed me for input on how the company could promote health and wellbeing in Latin America. I have not accomplished much for this cause. (No surprise, as I am an exercise scientist, not a businessman.) But I simply cannot shake the issue of worldwide hunger from my head.

What about you? Would you help? Consider the facts. In 2005-2006, there were more than seventy-two million obese people in the United States alone.[2] While there are no official numbers, the weight-loss industry is estimated to be a forty-billion-dollar per year business, and still growing.[3] The strategy of paying more money for less food is certainly not working to combat obesity (even if it is profitable for businesses): during the past twenty-five years, obesity has increased. According to *Morbidity and Mortality Weekly Report*, a publication from the U.S. Centers for Disease Control and Prevention, "overall, age-adjusted obesity rates were 15.6%, 19.8%, and 23.7% for the 1995, 2000, and 2005 surveys, respectively."[4]

Actually, what else would we expect? The economy dictates that all companies, including food companies, must strive to be ever more profitable—not simply to do well, but to do *better* year after year after year. To me as a consumer, that means that these companies must sell more and more food to a fixed number of people (or to convince those same people to pay more for the same amount of food). There seems to be no other way around it!

But what about all the millions who go hungry because they cannot afford food? Will they keep falling through the cracks of the system? I believe that a food company has the obligation to include hunger in the equation, and that it might even be able to do so at a profit. I would be willing to pay more for a "hunger-friendly" product, much the same way that many people are willing to pay for "environmentally sound" products. Those in the business world should be able to figure out how to make this work.

Here's another option: special offers. In Costa Rica, I am sure that there are many companies that allocate an important chunk of the advertising costs for their products to paying for big prizes. These prizes, or special offers, are expected to drive sales upward. The companies make all of us subsidize these promotions because, naturally, the cost of those promotions is built into the price of the products. This is supervised by the government and has a complicated set of rules and regulations governing it (or so I would like to believe).

What if those food companies chose to put that money into feeding the hungry instead? I believe that many consumers would prefer to buy a product from a company that guarantees to help feed the hungry and the needy, rather than buying a product from a company that will perhaps—and only remotely maybe—make them a winner. This "social conscience" or responsibility could be worth a lot in the marketplace and the money markets. If you have the skills and hold the right position in these companies, you could make this work.

> *What good is it, my brothers, if a man claims to have faith but has no deeds? Can such faith save him? Suppose a brother or sister is without clothes and daily food. If one of you says to him, "Go, I wish you well; keep warm and well fed," but does nothing about his physical needs, what good is it? In the same way, faith by itself, if it is not accompanied by action, is dead.*
>
> —James 2:14-17

JOURNEY 20

ANGELS?

HAVING A GUARDIAN angel is an attractive idea. In my child-hood days, when I had my share of night fears, I would pray regularly for my angel to protect me. While most of my fears at that time were unfounded, I can think of some real dangers during my travels that were averted, I am convinced, by divine intervention.

In February 2004, I rented a car to drive to Nicoya and Liberia, two cities in the Costa Rican North-Pacific, to meet with some soccer team coaches and players and prepare the ground for some field tests. The trip meant a total of nine to twelve hours of driving, but I was excited about the project and didn't mind the effort. The rental car was not luxurious, but it was comfortable. Among other things, it lacked power locks, which was something I did not think twice about at the time.

I took off for Nicoya and arrived on time, right before the practice. I left the car on the street near the stadium and went in to have my meetings. About an hour later, I came out, hopped in the car, and left for Liberia. I was still reflecting on how well the meetings had gone when a man who looked really familiar waved at me, signaling that I should slow down. I stopped right next to him and, to my surprise, he reached for the passenger door, opened it, and put his head in.

Contrary to my usual practice with my own car, all of the doors on the rental car—except mine—were unlocked! Of course, I did not know the man, even though he greeted me kindly with the familiar "¿cómo estás, *pura vida?*" and then asked, "What are you doing here in Nicoya?" He proceeded to ask me if I was going to Liberia (was that a coincidence?) and whether I could save him a trip there by giving him *X* amount of *colones* that the Fulano brothers ("those from the gas station") owed him. He said that I could get the money right back from them as soon as I arrived. Poor guy, the story was so hard to swallow…

The whole situation spelled "scam" and "danger." As the man spoke, I could not stop thinking that my wallet and cell phone were both right there on the passenger seat. I did not even have time to think or pray; I simply told him that I did not have any cash. God forgive me for the lie—it must have been so obvious to him from the thick wallet sitting right there on the front seat! But he looked at me, said, "Okay, see you around," pulled back and closed the door. I drove away before he could change his mind. I stopped a few blocks away to lock all the doors, thank God, and calm down.

Later that same year in July, my good friend Gary came to Costa Rica from Detroit. After he finished his short-term mission, we took a short vacation to Tivives in the Central Pacific. We had a wonderful time at the beach, swimming and mountain biking, and came back to San José the day before his flight back to the U.S.

Right before we arrived at my house, we stopped at a pharmacy to get some ibuprofen (mountain biking is a little hard on middle-aged men). We must have been there for less than five minutes. When we came out, we found one of the car windows broken and shattered glass all over our luggage. However, absolutely nothing was missing from the car. Gary's backpack, with his passport, driver's license, and money, was still sitting on the seat right next to the window. We were convinced that an angel scared the thief away before he could take anything. Nobody else was around.

The third story of divine intervention may hit a bit closer to home for the frequent traveler. During one of my trips, the man sitting next to me on the plane spilled his coffee in my direction, but the liquid evaporated instantly and never got to my laptop computer. I was as relieved as he was surprised! During another trip, this time to Mexico City, I spilled my drink on the traveler next to me who, unfortunately, did not have

ANGELS?

a guardian angel on duty. This businessman from Nicaragua got apple juice all over his shirt and pants, which abruptly ended my conversation with him. I hope he was carrying some spare clothes.

As Christians, we are not immune to mishaps, accidents, or robberies, but every now and then God likes to remind us that even the very hairs on our head are numbered (see Luke 12:7). Blessed are we when we are paying attention and can see God's hand in our lives.

For he will command his angels concerning you to guard you in all your ways.

—Psalm 91:11

Journey 21

Compassion for the
Masses

WHEN ONE HAS been raised with a reasonable amount of respect
and appreciation for other human beings, it is relatively easy (and
not particularly praiseworthy) to feel compassion for *one* elderly woman,
or *one* orphan, or *one* homeless person. The stirred emotions may even
be enough to move one to do something good for that person. But the
masses …well, that's another story. I find them simply overwhelming.

On the way to the airport, the highway is slow and there are too many
cars. Upon arrival, there are a series of lines for checking in, departure
border control, and security (incredibly long in São Paulo and Bogotá).
If you are lucky enough to receive preferential treatment in one line, the
other lines will compensate for it. When you finally make it to the gate,
it feels like whole armies are marching past you, in both directions, while
you wait to board. You get a better grasp of the word "masses" and feel
crushed by the attempt to feel compassion for them. "Competition" is
closer to the natural emotion that stirs in me.

Boarding itself is a "crowd experience." I guess doing it once a year
or so would not be so bad, but when you do it on a regular basis, it can
challenge your best manners. I could understand—but not appreciate—
the rush to get on the plane one particular time, many years back, in
Panama City. A smiling airline staffer announced over the microphone
that the plane was ready for boarding and that people could sit anywhere
they wanted. It must have been a practical joke! Everybody jumped

out of their seats and ran for the gate. I, of course, was working on my laptop, and by the time I had put it away, it was too late to fight for space. Sadly putting away my ticket marked "8-C," I boarded with the last of the passengers and sat in a middle seat way in the back of the aircraft. I can understand what happened on that occasion, but from the way people push and shove to get on the airplane, one would think it's free seating every time. Honestly, my experience boarding the subway in Tokyo was much better!

You will also struggle with the masses when you find a bus, not an airplane, at your gate. This is particularly maddening when you would gladly walk to your airplane some 50 or 100 meters away. Every time you think the driver should be closing the door and leaving, two or three more passengers will try to get in. I am convinced that there are bets on who can fit the most passengers in! Paradoxically, my only good experience riding a shuttle bus from the gate to the airplane was back in 1999 in Buenos Aires, when the driver was lost for a full thirty minutes trying to find the right aircraft. Most of the passengers were Argentines, and they spent the entire time making all kinds of jokes about how something like that could only happen in Argentina. I enjoyed the jokes and thought that the only reason the same thing could not happen in Costa Rica was that there would not be more than one airplane waiting for the passengers.

Jesus went through all the towns and villages, teaching in their synagogues, preaching the good news of the kingdom and healing every disease and sickness. When he saw the crowds, he had compassion on them, because they were harassed and helpless, like sheep without a shepherd. Then he said to his disciples, "The harvest is plentiful but the workers are few. Ask the Lord of the harvest, therefore, to send out workers into his harvest field."
—Matthew 9:35-38

Crowds are annoying during travel, but I continually remind myself that even though I do not know what is in each person's heart, many of the people I meet are harassed and helpless, like sheep without a shepherd. Instead of being annoyed, shouldn't I exercise some compassion and practice some intercession?

I keep on trying...

THE KNIGHT

HAVE YOU EVER imagined fighting in full armor? During a conference in Krakow, Poland, in September of 2004, our hosts organized a special dinner for the speakers and gave each of us a figurine of a knight about eight inches (20 cm) tall. We enjoyed a good meal at Wierzynek restaurant, and then our host stood up to speak. After I recovered from the shock of realizing that this huge, bearded, former Olympic rowing champion was kissing the speakers after thanking them and handing them a knight, I quickly thought of a polite excuse. "I apologize," I said, "but in Latin America it is not common for men to kiss each other." All those attending laughed politely, and I got my knight with a conventional handshake.

As I closely examined my nice replica, I wondered what it would be like to fight dressed up like that. Wearing armor must have been cumbersome, but it was the only way to fight in a battle without exposing your life. You could be more flexible and agile without it, but too vulnerable as well.

When I was single, I spent a few wonderful years with the Servants of the Word, an ecumenical, international Christian brotherhood of men living single for the Lord.[1] We had a regular lifestyle that required spending a considerable amount of time in prayer, Bible study, and fellowship, including shared meals and special celebrations. Although I often felt that this lifestyle was too structured and that it limited our ability to reach out, evangelize, and serve, it was clear to me that all of that was part of the armor. From our strength and stability, we were able to serve.

Let's now jump to the traveler. How much stuff is a person supposed to bring with him or her on a trip? I have experienced the extremes, from "fully armored" to "almost naked." (The latter occurred when I accidentally left without my wedding ring on a three-day trip.)

I used to have a large, hard, black suitcase that I called "the coffin." Back when the airlines allowed you to take up to seventy pounds per suitcase, I could carry a lot in that bag. I always looked sharp. I took gifts and books with me and brought back nice things from other countries. I began to consider giving up that suitcase after I could not make it fit into the trunk of my taxi in Buenos Aires. When the airlines lowered the weight limit to fifty pounds, that effectively put the nail in "the coffin."

On one-day trips I have had in the past, I have tried to travel with a computer backpack that includes my toothbrush, paper files, and no spare clothes. It feels wonderful to travel that light, but it's not so great if your return flight is cancelled and you have to stay overnight (which is a real possibility). This happened to me on February 13, 2002, when I flew from Costa Rica to Guatemala to give a one-hour presentation early in the afternoon. I was supposed to return that same night, but after the flight was delayed for about two hours and nothing seemed to be moving, we found out that the air traffic controllers had gone on strike! I was lucky enough to get a hotel nearby. I spent the following morning waiting at the airport, with wrinkled, smelly clothes and a wrinkled spirit. When I realized that it could be days before the strike was over, I called my hosts for help. They drove me to El Salvador (about five hours away), where I took an evening flight.

Ten years after I first started traveling regularly, I still strive to find the right balance between packing too much and packing too little—all the while adjusting to the increasingly ridiculous restrictions imposed by travel safety agencies. I try to remember that Jesus told His disciples to travel light (see Luke 9:1-3), while also considering that there are some things I should always bring with me on a trip. These include not only a passport, prescription medicine, and the tools for my business, but also those things that keep me safe and strong so I can fight the battle. In my case, I always bring my Bible, a good book for idle times, my Christian music, and three special tokens that I place on my night stand to remind me of my wife, my daughter, and my son.

> *Put on the full armor of God so that you can take your stand against the devil's schemes. For our struggle is not against flesh and blood, but against the rulers, against the authorities, against the powers of this dark world and against the spiritual forces of evil in the heavenly realms. Therefore put on the full armor of God, so that when the day of evil comes, you may be able to stand your ground, and after you have done everything, to stand. Stand firm then, with the belt of truth buckled around your waist, with the breastplate of righteousness in place, and with your feet fitted with the readiness that comes from the gospel of peace. In addition to all this, take up the shield of faith, with which you can extinguish all the flaming arrows of the evil one. Take the helmet of salvation and the sword of the Spirit, which is the word of God.*
>
> —Ephesians 6:11-17

JOURNEY 23

NOVELTY

W E ARE ALWAYS looking for something new. While we find
comfort in our routines, our senses always want new entertainment, new songs, new news. One thing about flying too often is that
although you know what to expect and how to work your way around
things, you also get the same airline magazine, the same movie, and,
sometimes, even the same flight attendant! That can get to be boring,
as it goes against our natural fondness for novelty.

The tendency to look for novelty is natural, but it can be counterpro-
ductive if it is not kept under control. It may even be a reason why some
people drift away from God. They keep looking for new experiences—a
new anointing, a fresh conversion, a new renewal—or they may have
too much curiosity about all the angel stories, or the Knights Templar,
or the new scrolls, or the Gospel of Judas.

There is an important place for sound doctrine, for orthodox
teaching, for tradition. Paul warns us about false teachers and, indirectly,
about novelty:

*For the time will come when men will not put up with sound doctrine.
Instead, to suit their own desires, they will gather around them a great
number of teachers to say what their itching ears want to hear. They will
turn their ears away from the truth and turn aside to myths.*
—2 Timothy 4:3-4

Most of us business travelers would not choose to fly a hot air balloon to our next business meeting just for a change, no matter how many times we may have boarded the same old flight. The same don't-search-for-novelty-just-for-the-sake-of-novelty logic should be applied to our lives and our relationship to God!

Stand at the crossroads and look; ask for the ancient paths, ask where the good way is, and walk in it, and you will find rest for your souls.
—Jeremiah 6:16

FOG

DURING MOST OF September, October, and November, you are likely to encounter a major problem when flying from Costa Rica: you cannot count on returning on the date you intended. After setting out on a business trip with a return date of the evening of October 9, 2005, the doubt once again emerged: *Will I get home tonight? Will the pilot be able to land the plane?* Out of my window, all I could see was rain pushed by the strong winds and the reflection of the navigation lights on a white sheet wrapped around the airplane.

My daughter, Ana Victoria, and I have many strong bonds, and a very special one is the fact that we both celebrate our birthdays on October 10. In fifteen years, only once have I not been home for the celebration. That was in October 1993, when I was in Ann Arbor doing data collection for my doctoral dissertation and my family was already back in Costa Rica. My daughter was only four years old at the time, but she remembers. Would this be the second time?

The problem is fog. It can get bad at the Juan Santamaría airport, and that, together with some technical limitations that have plagued the airport for years, can cause the authorities to close it and send all the flights to the Panama City or Liberia airports. Sometimes, this means arriving a full twenty-four hours later than you originally intended. In this case, those twenty-four hours meant a lot to me.

So often in life we feel as if we are flying through a sheet of fog. We fly by instruments. Like an airplane that cannot stop in midair, we keep going because we know we have to, but there is no reassuring scenery, no clear perspective, no encouraging signs along the way. The difficulty is not so much in the fog itself, but in the uncertainty of being able to reach our goal. If we only knew that we would make it home, we wouldn't mind the delays, the bumps, the multiple inconveniences.

It is especially hard to fly through fog if the pilots are silent just when we could use some words of comfort. God, however, does not forsake us. He guides us. He gives us His Word. He gives us His church.

Your word is a lamp to my feet and a light for my path.
—Psalm 119:105

My daughter, Ana Victoria, and I have many strong bonds, and a very special one is the fact that we both celebrate our birthdays on October 10. In sixteen years, only once have I not been home for the celebration...

Journey 25

Frustrated Plans

OUR PLANS ARE not God's plans. It was October 23, 2005, and I was in Caracas. I was waiting for my 4:30 p.m. flight back to Costa Rica when the announcement came over the intercom: "Passengers on TACA flight 630 to San José, your flight has been delayed. At this point we do not have a confirmed time of departure." I had given up going to Los Roques National Park, a beautiful set of islands on the Caribbean, so I could return home from my business trip on Sunday evening. In the end, I could have gone to the beach and made it back in time. It wouldn't have been a surprise to me if the flight—the only daily flight from Caracas to Costa Rica—had been cancelled and I ended up returning on Monday after all. Bummer...

I was reminded of Proverbs 16:9, "In his heart a man plans his course, but the LORD determines his steps," and Proverbs 19:21, "Many are the plans in a man's heart, but it is the Lord's purpose that prevails." Of course, the authors of these proverbs probably had in mind something more transcendent than a frustrated day at the beach, but I got the point anyway.

A couple of hours later, I was surprised to find out from an alert airline agent that the reason our flight had been delayed was because there had been a small plane accident at the Juan Santamaría Airport in Costa Rica. A small accident with a small plane had shut down our entire small airport for most of the day! The plane we were supposed to take had not even left Costa Rica yet, but in an unprecedented move, the airline had found another aircraft and a new crew. We would be ready to board as soon as the crew was notified that Juan Santamaría was open again.

My Los Roques disappointment and a possible twenty-four-hour delay turned into a manageable four-hour delay—just long enough for me to write this reflection!

> *Now listen, you who say, "Today or tomorrow we will go to this or that city, spend a year there, carry on business and make money," why, you do not even know what will happen tomorrow. What is your life? You are a mist that appears for a little while and then vanishes. Instead, you ought to say, "If it is the Lord's will, we will live and do this or that."*
> —James 4:13-15

ME TUBE

WHAT A BLESSING a good hotel room can be. At the same time, hotel rooms can pose certain challenges for people. For some, it is the noise next door or in the hallway. For others it may be the mini-bar. In my case, it is the distraction and temptations of a TV set. As Ravi Zacharias wrote, "Of all the possibilities to which we have recourse in entertainment, why are sensuality and violence the two most often used to titillate? Why not more healthy laughter? Why not more moral impetus? Why not more normative illustrations of what a home could be and should be? Why not more creative and legitimate entertainment rather than that which is destructive and offensive?"[1]

The later it is, and the more tired I am when I get back to the room after working, the likelier I will be to spend too much time channel surfing and watching what I would not watch at home. That shortens my resting hours, and I continue to be tired throughout the trip. Because of this—my spirit is willing, but my flesh is weak—I made the decision not to have a working TV set in my hotel room when I am traveling. This has been a real blessing, but it has not come without a fight.

Have you ever tried to ask for a room without a TV set? You can ask for a king-size bed, or a non-smoking room, or a down comforter, but try to get rid of the TV set in your room!

At first, my approach was not the best. I came to realize that the request was way too uncommon for the hotel staff, and oftentimes they would simply not cooperate. Here's a typical interaction:

Front desk: "How may I help you?"
Me: "Yes. I need to have the TV set removed from my room."
Front desk: "I beg your pardon? Is there something wrong with your TV?"
Me: "No, I just need to have it removed from my room."
Front desk: "Why? Do you need the space for something else?"
Me: "No. I just get too distracted when there is a TV in the room, and I have too much work to do."
Front desk: "Well, then, don't turn on the TV."
Me: "That is exactly my problem. I know I will turn it on. So please, would you remove it from my room?"

Whatever happened to "the customer is always right"? In the rare instance when I would get a technician to take care of the issue, he would not exactly be the happiest person in the world.

Then I realized that all I needed to do was to make sure that the TV was disabled. There are several ways to accomplish this. The easiest way is to remove the cable between the TV and the wall and take it to the reception person or the bell captain with clear instructions for him or her to keep it until you check out. This works well unless the hotel has installed a protecting cylinder, which will prevent you from detaching the cable (do people actually steal cable from hotel rooms?).

Some systems will not work without a remote control. In that case, you can take the remote control to the bell captain, or simply remove the batteries and throw them away in a waste basket in the lobby.

Some of these efforts fail when the hotel has "selective good service," such as the Ritz-Carlton, where they did not honor my request to have the TV set removed from the room. When the housekeeping woman was unable to turn on the guest-disabled TV for me, she made sure to get a replacement cable and get it in working order immediately.

If you are blessed enough to have a travel agency arranging your trip and they give you the opportunity to list any special requests such as "vegetarian meals" or "wheel-chair accessible," it is always a nice challenge for the staff when you write down, "No TV set in the room, please." So far, I have had about a 50 percent success rate with this approach. In addition to protecting myself, this is a good way to tell a good agent from a sloppy one!

When a travel agent is not involved, or when that approach has failed, a kind, patient effort with the hotel front desk staff is usually effective. By clearly stating that you need to have the TV set disabled instead of removed, you can avoid making it look like you are absolutely weird and are making irrational demands (okay, so you only look a bit weird). One time, a receptionist said, "Okay, I understand." I was afraid that he was simply being polite, but he took care of the issue.

Whatever approach I use, I always make sure that these efforts take place as early as possible, before I get too tired to fight. I know my weakness, and I have decided to do something about it. I want to have God, not the Tube, shape my mind.

Therefore, I urge you, brothers, in view of God's mercy, to offer your bodies as living sacrifices, holy and pleasing to God—this is your spiritual act of worship. Do not conform any longer to the pattern of this world, but be transformed by the renewing of your mind. Then you will be able to test and approve what God's will is—his good, pleasing and perfect will.
—Romans 12:1-2

CARS

I LIKE CARS so much that sometimes I think I should have been born in the U.S., the "automobile-paradise-on-earth." I have been a subscriber to *Consumer Reports* for more than fifteen years, and I always read the whole section on cars. I can tell the brand and model of almost any car at first sight. But in my country, we pay more than 50 percent in taxes for a new car, and then close to a 3 percent tax every year for the right to be stuck in traffic a few hours a week and bounce from pothole to pothole (the so-called "circulation/flow" permit). Add in the cost of insurance, and a new car is almost as expensive as a small house!

In this context, I was blessed with a great car. As I previously mentioned, back in 1990 my family and I moved from Costa Rica to Ann Arbor, Michigan, so that I could attend graduate school. We arrived with four suitcases, a three-year scholarship, and $12,000 in the bank. Among many other concerns, we needed to find an inexpensive car that we could drive for two years. Then we could buy Our Car: according to Costa Rican law, we could take a car back home *tax free*.[1] We drove an old car for about a year, occasionally stopping by the Suzuki dealership on Washtenaw Avenue to admire the brand new Sidekicks that met all our needs. When the old car died a year too soon, we didn't hesitate to go and negotiate our brand-new 1991 car for $10,750.

In 1993, we moved back home and brought the car back with us. It remained our only car for seven years and our main family car for more than ten years. We went to so many corners of Costa Rica in our Suzuki Sidekick! When it reached 100,000 miles, we went out as a family and had a special thanksgiving celebration. After having it for 16½ years, we sold it for six thousand dollars. It was difficult, but the time had come to part ways.

My fondness of cars, therefore, does not translate into collecting them, as some millionaires do. It doesn't translate into changing cars every year, not even every three years, as would be normal for many middle-class people in the U.S. In my case, I always look forward to renting a car: midsize and non-smoking. With those requirements, I have driven a wide variety of cars during my business trips. I always compare the gadgets, special designs and transmission systems in each, dreaming I am shopping for a new car. I also get the opportunity to be grateful.

In January 2006, I went to Chicago on a business trip. The poor Saturn Ion I ended up with had everything going against it. I arrived at 10:30 p.m. and then had to wait in the wind for fifteen minutes before the shuttle bus to the rental car lot arrived. When I got there, the car was in the far end of the parking lot, and it was not even turned on. I realize that it should have been much colder for January in Chicago, but for someone who lives in the tropics, it was cold enough. I could not figure out how to open the car trunk, so I had to pull out the keys from the ignition to open it manually. After loading my luggage and taking the driver's seat, I dropped the keys in exactly the wrong spot. It took me fifteen minutes of fumbling, a large dose of self-control, and one cut finger to finally pull them out of a narrow opening between my seat and the center console. My bias was not assisted by the poor finish, weak engine, and overall "basicness" of the car.

My trip in February was a totally different story. My flight landed on time at nine p.m., the shuttle bus was right there after I picked up my luggage, the car was warm when I got to the parking lot, the vehicle was a brand-new SUV—a Ford Escape Limited—with 250 miles on it, and it all came for the price of a midsize regular car. What a difference! The contrast with my previous rental (same company) was so clear that it made me think: *Which one did I deserve?*

When you are a frequent traveler and you have reached "elite" status in some frequent flyer and hotel programs, you come to believe that you *deserve* perfect attention. If you don't get a requested upgrade, you feel that you are being cheated. If a cancelled flight forces you to stay overnight at the airport hotel and they place you in a room only ten feet away from a construction crew that starts their remodeling work at six a.m., you strongly complain, realizing that not only are you not getting what you deserve, but also that if you don't look after yourself, nobody else will.

The danger of all this is that it's too easy to forget about gratitude. Which car did I deserve to get at the rental company? In life in general, if I really got what I deserved, I know where I would be. I know that the wages of sin is death (see Romans 6:23). I know that it is by God's grace that I am forgiven; it is by His grace that I can come to Him every day in prayer. And when I travel and don't get what I would like to have—such as an upgrade or a hot meal on the plane or a quiet room—I can still thank God because of His constant reminders to be grateful.

> *The LORD is compassionate and gracious,*
> *slow to anger, abounding in love.*
> *He will not always accuse, nor will he harbor his anger forever;*
> *he does not treat us as our sins deserve*
> *or repay us according to our iniquities.*
> *For as high as the heavens are above the earth,*
> *so great is his love for those who fear him;*
> *As far as the east is from the west,*
> *so far has he removed our transgressions from us.*
> *As a father has compassion on his children,*
> *so the LORD has compassion on those who fear him;*
> *for he knows how we are formed,*
> *he remembers that we are dust.*
>
> —Psalm 103:8-14

STUCK INSIDE AN AIRPLANE

THERE MUST BE something we can do, right? It is Monday, May 29, 2006, and the day has started early and well. My drive back from McMaster University has gone incredibly smoothly. I had spent a couple of days there attending a celebration of life in memory of Dr. Oded Bar-Or, a dear friend and colleague. I had returned the rental car, checked in for my flight, and cleared U.S. immigration and customs even before leaving Canada.

But now, I've been inside the airplane for three-and-a-half hours, a full 210 minutes, waiting for authorization to take off from Toronto to Chicago O'Hare. The day is unseasonably hot, and it is too warm and uncomfortable in the cabin. The babies are crying. The mothers are crying. The fathers feel like crying, but they have chosen to argue with the flight attendants instead. Something *must* be done. We are trapped.

You often might feel the same way at difficult points in your life. The feeling is horrible: you feel compelled to do something, and yet you are convinced that whatever you do will probably only make matters worse. The only way out is to follow the example of Paul the apostle, and pray.

Paul and Silas had been thrown in prison in Philippi after being stripped and beaten harshly because of the complaints of the owners of a slave girl whom they had delivered from a spirit. They were put in a secure cell, their feet carefully locked in shackles. Talk about being trapped. "About midnight Paul and Silas were praying and singing hymns to God, and the other prisoners were listening to them. Suddenly there was such a violent earthquake that the foundations of the prison were shaken. At once all the prison doors flew open, and everybody's chains came loose" (Acts 16:25-26).

Elizabeth Goodine must have been strongly inspired by this story when she wrote the song "I Bless Your Name." The words, as interpreted by the group Selah, resonate in my mind:

> *Some midnight hour*
> *If you should find*
> *You're in a prison in your mind*
> *Reach out and praise*
> *Defy those chains*
> *And they will fall*
> *In Jesus' Name.*[1]

A woman's voice in front of me interrupts my thoughts. "How can you work on your computer with this heat?" she asks. I wish I had been praying. I was only recording my thoughts for this section. Inspiration comes when it comes.

> *In my anguish I cried to the LORD,*
> *and he answered by setting me free.*
> —Psalm 118:5

Journey 29

Awards Banquet

EVERY YEAR I try to attend the annual meeting of the American College of Sports Medicine. During this conference there is a banquet that I sometimes attend, at which time a few colleagues receive awards for their accomplishments. Invariably, there is one or two who will say, "Thank you to my wife and my children, whom I sacrificed for ten years so I could devote time to working on this project…"

Is it worth it? Are our priorities right when we sacrifice our family for worldly goals? I don't think so. Even if the goal is something noble and good, it should not take priority over our major responsibility: our family. If I ever accomplish something important, I want to be able to say that I thank God because I did not have to sacrifice my family in order to do this or that. Instead, it was something we could do together. They had enough sacrifices to make because I was traveling so much.

But seek first his kingdom and his righteousness, and all these things will be given to you as well.

—Matthew 6:33

A DIFFERENT PERSPECTIVE

I WAS RETURNING from Chicago on June 23, 2006, and my plane into Dallas was ninety minutes late. I had only ten minutes to get to my gate, D14. I knew that sprinting to make the connection was not a good idea; if I jogged there, steady, without stops, I might make it. I was almost there when…bam! A security guard stopped me. No explanations; it was simply a well-coordinated procedure, securing an area of a half-dozen gates. I tried to go around from the other side, but my gate was among those secured. My brain began to work as fast as possible, exploring my other options. I couldn't miss my flight to Costa Rica or I would be stuck in Dallas for twenty-four hours! So close…

But what if there was a bomb threat? In that instance, would I rather be on the plane or standing in the hallway as a spectator? That possibility can certainly change your perspective.

Our perspective on things is so narrow, so immediate, and so limited in every way. On the one hand, it is fair to say that we must regularly act on the information that we have available. If we always tried to ponder all the possibilities and gather additional information, we would be paralyzed. On the other hand, we must always remember who we are as sons and daughters of God. We have to remember that He does have a perfect plan. His perspective is complete.

We may understand some things instantly, while others may have to wait for a few years. Such was the case back in June 1981 when I received a letter from the German academic exchange agency DAAD telling me, to my great disappointment, that my doctoral scholarship had been cancelled (two months before traveling to Germany to get started) without any further explanation. One year later, after my appeal was resolved in my favor, I spent a week in prayer and fasting and decided to turn down the scholarship. God had done many amazing things in my life during those months.

I was thankful for not being in Germany, but one thing didn't fit quite right: Why had the case been resolved in my favor? Then one day in the fall of 1985, while talking to a Christian brother about the experience, he very naturally said to me, "Isn't it great how God gave you the opportunity to give up your studies in Germany when you were ready to do it?" At that point, everything fell into place.

There are some things that we will never understand, but it truly helps to trust in our Father, who knows better than anyone what is good for us. He has a perfect, eternal, multi-planar 360-degree perspective.

"Once again, passengers on American flight 2167 to San Ho-Say, Coustu Rica, this is your last call." Security was removing all the yellow tape. I rushed to the gate. I never did find out why they had closed the area for thirty minutes.

To man belong the plans of the heart,
but from the LORD comes the reply of the tongue.
All a man's ways seem innocent to him,
but motives are weighed by the LORD.
Commit to the LORD whatever you do,
and your plans will succeed.
The LORD works out everything for his own ends—
even the wicked for a day of disaster

—Proverbs 16:1-4

A Different Perspective

*"For my thoughts are not your thoughts,
neither are your ways my ways,"
declares the LORD.
"As the heavens are higher than the earth,
so are my ways higher than your ways
and my thoughts than your thoughts."*

—Isaiah 55:8-9

Oh, the depth of the riches of the wisdom and knowledge of God! How unsearchable his judgments, and his paths beyond tracing out! "Who has known the mind of the Lord? Or who has been his counselor?"

—Romans 11:33-34

JOURNEY 31

THE RIGHT CHOICE

I T IS SATURDAY, September 9, 2006. I have finished my work responsibilities in Bogotá, Colombia, and my flight is not leaving until Sunday afternoon. This morning, we will go on a tour of the city, have a free afternoon after lunch, and then have a final dinner with our hosts. After this, I will be on my own until tomorrow. So why shouldn't I try to change my flight to today?

My wife doesn't like it when I change my plans, even if it means my returning home a bit earlier and being there to support her tasks with our children. Deep down inside, she fights a fear that I may have an accident or that something will go wrong. Whenever there is an air crash, you always hear stories about people who were supposed to be on the plane but were not and others who ended up there at the last minute. Of course, there is no way that anyone could have known which group he or she would be in, but every time I make a change, I really think about it.

This time, however, I have a good reason to leave Bogotá: I know myself. I know that being alone, tired, and without anything to do (except working more) places me in a dangerous spiritual position. Such conditions are fertile ground for temptations, and on this trip I have been fighting temptation. Upon arrival, I had already requested that my TV set be removed from the room, but that might not be enough. Now I want to be home with my family in a safer environment. I have prayed hard during this trip, and I want to honor God.

89

Now it's Saturday evening, and I am in Costa Rica. It was hard to change my travel arrangements. I had to pay a fee to the airline, I arrived late at the airport, I had no time to claim the $52 airport tax exemption, the lines for check-in were very long, and I barely caught my flight. Several times I wondered if I had made the right choice. However, any doubts disappeared, at least momentarily, when I called home from the airplane and my daughter answered and said, "That is wonderful, Papa, you are coming a full day early!"

Now I am in Costa Rica indeed, but I am still inside the airplane. We are parked at the Liberia International Airport, where the aircraft is being refueled. We could not land at our destination in San José because of bad weather. When the captain made a failed approach at the Juan Santamaría airport more than ninety minutes ago, my doubts resurfaced. Did I make the right decision? How many more hours will I have to be stuck inside this airplane?

We don't make decisions knowing what the results will be. No, we make them using the best information available at the time and then trust that God will see us through the consequences. I made the right decision because I needed to protect my heart, and I tried to get home earlier to be with my family. Blessed be God, the rest is in His hands.

But Daniel resolved not to defile himself with the royal food and wine, and he asked the chief official for permission not to defile himself this way. Now God had caused the official to show favor and sympathy to Daniel, but the official told Daniel, "I am afraid of my lord the king, who has assigned your food and drink. Why should he see you looking worse than the other young men your age? The king would then have my head because of you."

Daniel then said to the guard whom the chief official had appointed over Daniel, Hananiah, Mishael and Azariah, "Please test your servants for ten days: Give us nothing but vegetables to eat and water to drink. Then compare our appearance with that of the young men who eat the royal food, and treat your servants in accordance with what you see."

—Daniel 1:8-13

BETTER IS ONE DAY IN YOUR COURTS

ACCORDING TO MY wife, I have three types of business trips: (1) those that are mandatory, (2) those that are a good thing to do, and (3) those that I choose to do because of personal reasons, but which are clearly optional. Because in the past six years I have had to travel more than my family and I would like, I have tried to limit the number of the latter to the bare minimum, even though there is always a business purpose in them. Now I am in the middle of one of those optional trips, and I keep thinking, *What in the world am I doing here? Should I really have taken this trip?*

As I write, my sister-in-law is dying. She was diagnosed with a brain tumor eleven months ago, and after a long and trying illness, she is ready to meet her Lord. Our entire extended family has been closely involved, caring for her, supporting my brother and their four children, and praying constantly for God's will to be done. When I committed myself to this trip, I never imagined my departure would coincide with the announcement that her death was imminent. By then, it was too late to back out. So I left for the airport, boarded a plane, and eighteen hours later was arriving at my hotel in London.

Shortly before leaving, I received an e-mail that read, "I apologize for the delay in getting Luis's schedule for London to you, but, as you may know, commercial production schedules are very difficult to figure out. We will be using Luis as the featured scientist in our soccer scenario, which will be filmed on Thursday. The way our shooting schedule breaks down now, we will only need one GSSI scientist per sport, and soccer will only take one day of filming. Therefore, if Luis would like, *he can arrive in London as late as Wednesday instead of Monday.* However, if Luis would still like to come to London on Monday to see the city, take care of other business, and so forth, we will still pay for his accommodations and expenses for the planned days. Please let me know what he would like to do so that we can plan for it." Oh boy. It was too late to change my plans to take advantage of this opportunity. The message only made matters worse.

So, here I am, away from home, working on my computer in the hotel room. Some days, knowing that I am walking in God's will feels particularly important. Oh, God, this is such a day, and I am almost certain that I am not walking in Your will!

Two days after writing the lines above—cutting my trip short because of my sister-in-law's death—I had the opportunity to share the gospel with Barty, the young London driver who was curious about my "religiousity." Perhaps one day I will find out whether this was God's way of writing straight on crooked lines or if He had intended me to be in London all along.

Better is one day in your courts than a thousand elsewhere; I would rather be a doorkeeper in the house of my God than dwell in the tents of the wicked. For the Lord God is a sun and shield; the Lord bestows favor and honor; no good thing does he withhold from those whose walk [travel] is blameless. O Lord Almighty, blessed is the man who trusts in you.
—Psalm 84:10-12

YOUR RIGHT HAND HOLDS ME FAST

I RAN INTO Meg at the San José airport. She had her two children securely tied with a strap to her wrist. I am sure that Meg is a wonderful mother, but she does not trust her ability to control her children in an airport. I wish these things had existed when I was a kid...or do I? Life would have been a bit less interesting, but I could have saved my mother a few scares, not to mention a few frights of my own.

As a child I was lost at least three times that I can remember, all of them in large crowds. I was also lost in the Osa Peninsula in the Costa Rican South Pacific jungle for a couple of hours, but by that time I was almost ten years old (in my own eyes, almost a man!), and my father was with me. Although he was also lost, I felt I could face anything because he was holding my hand. I was safe, much like Meg's children must have felt at the airport.

Today, my Father holds me by my right hand. I am always with Him. He leads me to peaceful waters and guides me in paths of righteousness. He stills the storm and comforts me every step of the way. He alone is my rock and my salvation; He is my fortress, and I will not be shaken. Though my heart and my flesh should waste away, God is my rock, my portion forever.

On my bed I remember you; I think of you through the watches of the night. Because you are my help, I sing in the shadow of your wings. My soul clings to you; your right hand upholds me.

—Psalm 63:6-8

BUT FOR THE GRACE OF GOD (THIS JUST CAN'T BE HAPPENING) ᥱ᷎᷍

I T WAS DECEMBER 17, 2006. It had been a difficult year, with many challenges and work-related issues. I thought my international travel schedule had been easier, but my calendar didn't lie: I had spent ninety-six days overseas, which was slightly above my self-imposed limit of no more than 25 percent of the days in the year. My last trip to the airport that year should have been very different, as Ana María and I were dropping our daughter off to spend two weeks with relatives in Neenah, Wisconsin.

At the airport, I realized how spoiled I was due to my frequent traveler status, because it took my daughter ninety minutes to do the check-in as a regular passenger, compared to my typical twenty minutes. But by 8:30 a.m., we were ready to leave the airport and do the sixty-minute drive back home. No more airports until 2007!

At one p.m., the phone rang at our home. It was our daughter, calling collect. I was thankful, because I had asked her to call us as soon as she arrived in Atlanta for her mother's—and her father's—peace of mind. However, as it turned out, she was still in Costa Rica. Her flight had been delayed for three hours and then cancelled, and there was no further information available at this point. One hour later, she called again to tell us that the airline might be able to put her on another flight at three p.m., but she would miss the last flight out of Atlanta and would have to spend the night somewhere near the airport. We told her to go stand in line and wait for us. After another sixty-minute drive to the airport, we found her standing in line with her luggage. Everyone on the plane had been told to pick up their luggage and go back to the counters to make alternative arrangements.

At this point, my flesh began to rebel ardently. *They have no right to do this! Not to me. This is Sunday! We are supposed to rest. I am* not *supposed to endure another single minute of airport aggravation. I am supposed to be done for the rest of the year!* But it really wasn't a matter of what I was feeling at that moment. My teenage daughter had been standing in lines and waiting inside an airplane since seven a.m., with nothing to eat or drink. I had to take over, though I had no energy left in me to do so. If I allowed my flesh to win out, I could hit someone, or insult someone, or simply shout "bomb" out loud and get myself arrested—or worse. So, once again, I asked God for patience and energy to face life. I joined my daughter in line, where we waited for two hours until we were finally able to get her flights rearranged for the next day.

God does not waste any opportunity to help us grow in patience in the Holy Spirit, as He knows that patience will be required for things that are much more important in life than just a few hassles at an airport.

> *And the Lord's servant must not quarrel; instead, he must be kind [patient] to everyone, able to teach, not resentful. Those who oppose him he must gently instruct, in the hope that God will grant them repentance leading them to a knowledge of the truth, and that they will come to their senses and escape from the trap of the devil who has taken them captive to do his will.*
>
> —2 Timothy 2:24-26

BLINDED BY THE LIGHT

I T HAD BEEN more than five years since I had first started doing tests with professional athletes. So what was the big deal in this case? And what was with all of the lights? With all of that equipment, we ran the risk of not having enough power for our treadmill. No treadmill meant no test, and no test meant no documentary.

Our first efforts to schedule tests with Ronaldinho dated back to 2004. For years we had been trying to get him to agree to perform the tests in our labs not far from Chicago, but his schedule was a real nightmare. His regular training and Spanish tournament games with F.C. Barcelona, European tournament games with F.C. Barcelona, and occasional practice and games with the Brazilian national team all meant that when he had a few days off, he truly wanted to be off. How could we then get him to spare three full days to fly across the Atlantic to do a couple of hours of testing in Chicago?

For those readers not familiar with football (soccer), Ronaldinho had been officially recognized as the best soccer player in the world by different organizations at different times. The possibility of doing some testing with him was like being given the opportunity to do testing with Michael Jordan back in the 1990s. The most important part about this particular test was to evaluate Ronaldinho's sweat rate when he was exercising in moderate heat stress and to analyze the composition of his sweat. From the data, we could prepare recommendations for him on fluid and nutrient intake and also create some brochures and videos to help educate athletes on how to prevent dehydration and other heat-related illnesses in sports. Getting the data was important, but so was getting the right images—hence the importance of the lights!

We finally had to give up on our idea of testing at our Chicago headquarters and agree to work at a cooperating laboratory at the University of Castilla La Mancha in Toledo, Spain, which was only a few hours away from Barcelona. So this test, which had finally been scheduled for February 12, 2007, and then postponed to March 15, 2007, was in fact a big deal.

Both the still photographers and the video photographers were true professionals. They knew how to shine the right lights on the star of the test, as so many other professionals do in the arts and journalism. Yet as much as I respected Ronaldinho's athletic abilities and his kind demeanor, I kept reminding myself that he was just an idol—one who could not truly shine on his own.

Any lights shining on the wrong subject will mislead you (and the star, too, as most times the star of the show is blinded and cannot even see his audience). I focus on my Lord Jesus, the true light that enlightens every man. He does not blind me, dazzle me, or confuse me. He shines on my path to show me the way, shines on my thoughts to show me the truth, and shines on my life to lead me to Life, because He is the way, the truth, and the life. His light shines in the darkness, and the darkness cannot resist it. John the Baptist "came as a witness to testify concerning that light, so that through him all men might believe. He himself was not the light; he came only as a witness to the light. The true light that gives light to every man was coming into the world" (John 1:7-9).

May I, like John the Baptist, be a witness to the one true light.

CONTENTMENT

I KNOW HOW it feels to be separated from God the Father. I hope I will never have to go through it again. In the words of a song based on Isaiah 54, "For a brief moment I abandoned you, my wrath went forth, I hid my face from you. But with steadfast love I shall call you back, the God of Israel shall be your savior."[1]

On one business trip, my wife called me to say, "Luis Fer, we have a problem. Esteban is seriously missing you, and it hasn't even been a week since you left. Last night he cried a lot before going to sleep. He wanted you to come back immediately. I need you to talk to him tomorrow." I took steps to secure Internet access the next day so that I could have a videoconference with him.

I returned home three days later, arriving at ten p.m. Esteban was crying, awake way past his usual bed time of 7:30 p.m. I lay in bed with him for a while. It worked like magic: he was asleep within ten minutes. Early the next morning while I was praying, he knocked on my door, walked in, and sat next to me. He was delighted simply to be with his father.

Esteban reminded me that there is no place where I feel more at home than next to my Father. And He is never away on business travel!

My heart is not proud, O Lord, my eyes are not haughty; I do not concern myself with great matters or things too wonderful for me. But I have stilled and quieted my soul; like a weaned child with its mother, like a weaned child is my soul within me. O Israel, put your hope in the Lord both now and forevermore.

—Psalm 131:1-3

Journey 37

Yet Another Way to Feel Useless

On June 1, 2006, I was feeling frustrated. I had tried to schedule an appointment at the Focus on the Family headquarters in Colorado Springs, Colorado, to try and promote the ideas in this book. I had no appointment yet, but I was arriving a full day early to the American College of Sports Medicine annual meeting in Denver so I could go to Colorado Springs and, at the very least, make some contacts. Well, a big mess at O'Hare wrecked my plans, making me arrive almost twenty hours later than I had originally planned. I did not even have time to show up at the door, uninvited, at Focus on the Family. What was God trying to tell me? It was clear to me that this book had to be something *He* did, not me. But I had been absolutely dry, with no ideas at all, for more than two months at that point.

It is now September 20, 2007. The inspiration for this book came to me almost *two years ago*. At that time, I thought I could finish it in a few months, but twenty-four months hardly qualifies as "a few." God has been teaching me all this time, the hard way, that He wants to do this in His own timeframe. I thought I had nothing against God's timing when we started, but now I'm not so sure. I guess He knows me better and sees many things in me that need to be fixed first, such as relying too much on my own strength and resources.

It is *so* hard for me to rely 100 percent upon the Lord! I need to be organized and efficient to function in life, and it is all too easy for me to get caught up in my own plans and assume that I can do everything I plan. In fact, I believe people could not function if they did not start from the assumption that their plans were going to work. But then, we need to have the flexibility to adjust when they don't. That's where I have a hard time.

When traveling, for instance, I am forced to put the control in the hands of others, such as the airlines, the hotels, and the taxi drivers, and too many things can go wrong. Delays are common, but the real problem is not the delay itself: it is the lack of control and the feeling that there is nothing I can do about it. ("If only they had told me that the flight was going to leave two hours late, I would have gone to the restaurant to eat a decent meal instead of waiting at the gate!") I find it particularly difficult to function, think clearly, and use my time wisely under total uncertainty. I can't help but feel useless, and I get really impatient.

Who said "control freak"?

> *Be patient, then, brothers, until the Lord's coming. See how the farmer waits for the land to yield its valuable crop and how patient he is for the autumn and spring rains. You too, be patient and stand firm, because the Lord's coming is near.*
>
> —James 5:7-8

MY BEST FRIEND GAVE
ME A GUN

A S I WRITE this, I am sitting in my hotel room in Palatine, Illinois, near the Gatorade® Sports Science Institute headquarters in Barrington. I recently celebrated ten years of consulting for the GSSI. When I started back in 1997, my best friend (I will call him Newton) had recently moved to Lake Geneva, Wisconsin, about a ninety-minute drive from the GSSI headquarters. What a blessing! I could spend time with him every time I came to Barrington. I never could imagine why God was giving us that opportunity.

Newton had been going through a difficult time with his family. His wife had developed encephalitis while they were serving as Christian missionaries in Costa Rica and had not recovered for about nine years. This made their lives very tough and challenging. I had been supporting them regularly during those years, praying constantly for them, meeting with Newton to talk and pray whenever possible, and even offering to be his accountability partner. Finally, they decided to move back to the Chicago area, her home city, where she could hopefully recover.

During one of my visits to Barrington, Newton called me and told me that he had a gift for me. He wanted to give me a gun. A gun? For me? The most dangerous weapon I had ever owned was a two-inch switchblade (which was dangerous mostly because of the risk of accidental self-inflicted wounds!).

When I asked Newton about the gift, he said, "I have always wanted to give you a gun, and I was recently able to find this old pistol that does not work. Please accept it. It represents what you did for me. When I confessed to you how I had kept on living a sinful life for several years, deceiving and concealing all my wrongdoing, you had every right to walk away. I had betrayed your trust. I had made you waste your time. I had handed you a loaded gun that was pointed at my head, and my future literally depended on what you chose to do with my confession. You could have pulled the trigger, condemning me. But you chose to forgive me, throwing the gun away and giving me a chance to live." So I accepted the gun and took it back to my home in Costa Rica.[1]

Indeed, Newton had had several affairs with married and unmarried women while his wife was ill, something that eventually cost him his marriage and caused a significant amount of pain to his family. He had lied about it to everyone close to him. After a suggestion from his wife, he had agreed to go to an addiction center, where he spent many days facing the harsh truth about his actions and learned how to break free. He prepared a written confession, which he shared with only two people before destroying it: his wife and me.

How could I not forgive him? On the one hand, the fault had been so serious that it ended up destroying his marriage; but on the other hand, I knew my own heart. I knew how many times I had needed forgiveness from God. I knew all too well how He taught us to pray, "Forgive us our debts, as we also have forgiven our debtors" (Matthew 6:12). I did not want to be like the servant who, after being forgiven millions of dollars in debt by his master, refused to forgive his fellow servant for a few dollars and had him thrown in jail (see Matthew 18:23-35). Besides, I knew that God had forgiven Newton already, so who was I to condemn him? I begged for God's grace and did my part.

The following nine years we had at least a dozen deep-dish pizzas at Giordano's. We shared our dreams and challenges, we prayed together, and we went shopping together in the Barrington area. God worked in my heart to allow me to forgive Newton completely—so much so, in fact, that I have never thought of holding that old gun to Newton's head again.

Therefore, the kingdom of heaven is like a king who wanted to settle accounts with his servants. As he began the settlement, a man who owed him ten thousand talents was brought to him. Since he was not able to pay, the master ordered that he and his wife and his children and all that he had be sold to repay the debt. The servant fell on his knees before him. "Be patient with me," he begged, "and I will pay back everything." The servant's master took pity on him, canceled the debt and let him go. But when that servant went out, he found one of his fellow servants who owed him a hundred denarii. He grabbed him and began to choke him. "Pay back what you owe me!" he demanded. His fellow servant fell to his knees and begged him, "Be patient with me, and I will pay you back." But he refused. Instead, he went off and had the man thrown into prison until he could pay the debt. When the other servants saw what had happened, they were greatly distressed and went and told their master everything that had happened. Then the master called the servant in. "You wicked servant," he said, "I canceled all that debt of yours because you begged me to. Shouldn't you have had mercy on your fellow servant just as I had on you?" In anger his master turned him over to the jailers to be tortured, until he should pay back all he owed. This is how my heavenly Father will treat each of you unless you forgive your brother from your heart.

—Matthew 18:23-35

STAY IN SHAPE

M ORE AND MORE, health authorities are insisting on regular exercise as an important component of a healthy lifestyle. Having endured mocking from friends, family, and neighbors when I started jogging at the age of 16, it's nice to hear that I was right all along. I have enjoyed leading a physically active lifestyle throughout my life, not excelling in any particular sport but being fit and skilled enough to enjoy a wide variety of recreational sports.

As an exercise scientist, I am committed to regular physical activity, but I have experienced firsthand how business trips can create a number of conflicts with an exercise program. During my first year of frequent travel, my discipline and exercise routines became a liability instead of an asset due to my high standards and expectations. My normal daily workouts were at least one hour long (occasionally two), they included a good warm-up before the aerobic training and a good stretching segment at the end, and my fitness club facilities were state of the art. During travel, I encountered tight agendas, incredibly poor hotel fitness facilities, and very limited options. As a result, on most trips I would not exercise.

I quickly learned that a costly hotel may not have adequate fitness facilities (or no facilities at all); that hotel managers' standards for fitness facilities can be ten to twenty (and even thirty) years behind the times; that hotel pools tend to be two to three feet deep; that running in the streets in the United Kingdom can be *very* dangerous, as you tend to look the wrong way before crossing a street; that the combination of altitude and pollution make it a bad idea to run hard in Mexico City; that Bogotá is friendly to runners, inline skaters, and cyclists while Caracas and San José are definitely not; that the fanciest hotels may open their fitness facilities one or two hours later than indicated in the guest information binder; that hotels often consider their fitness facility an additional source of revenue rather than a service to their guests; and that when a hotel is remodeling its fitness facility, it may not feel it is necessary to let you know in advance or provide an alternative.

I paid dearly to learn that many hotels in Latin America have fire doors that lock behind you once you exit to exercise in the stairway and that the only way back is out the lower level into the street; that it is not a good idea to get lost while running in Cleveland in the winter; that those purple-blue bubbles you see floating in the ocean in Key Biscayne belong to the famous Portuguese men-of-war that you read about in lifeguard training textbooks; that people all over the world tend to underestimate distances when you are the one doing the walking or the cycling; that mid-priced mountain bike rentals are not meant to be taken mountain biking; that sometimes the "streams" you encounter while running on the beach are sewage; that pizza delivery is always late except that one evening you cleverly order it before going to the gym for a 30-minute workout; and that there must always be exercise gear in your carry-on luggage–not only your prescription medicine and business clothes–for those occasions when your checked luggage doesn't arrive with you.

Naturally, I am talking about things that I have experienced during many years of travel. I previously mentioned that for me the first year of business travel was the worst, but I persevered and started applying a few important tricks:

- Make sure to include time for exercise in your daily schedule, and make it clear to your hosts that you need that time.
- Be flexible. If you only have thirty minutes available for exercise, then exercise for twenty minutes and take a quick shower. That is better than having no exercise at all.

- Take notes on fitness facilities at the hotels you visit, just in case you come back to the same city.
- Learn a basic exercise routine that you can do in your bedroom.
- Use the hotel stairs, not the elevator, whenever possible (and only if it is safe to do so).
- Always bring a swimming suit and goggles with you (they don't take much extra space in your luggage).
- Build exercise into your daily commitments. Walk to and from meetings whenever it is reasonable and safe to do so. When sightseeing, don't just look at the structures from a distance, but take the time to go and explore them (for instance, I have climbed the pyramids at Teotihuacán, Mexico, and the hills at Poços de Caldas, Brazil). Sign up for sports activities at your meetings (I always try to take part in the Gisolfi 5K fun run/walk at the annual American College of Sports Medicine conference). If you are in charge of an event, organize physically active socializing into the program, such as a city tour on bicycles instead of visiting a museum.[1]

By including at least some exercise or physical activity into all my trips, I have been able to stay fit, maintain a healthy and balanced life, and be a good steward of my body. My focus, however, is not to train like an athlete, but to keep my priorities straight.

Rather, train yourself to be godly. For physical training is of some value, but godliness has value for all things, holding promise for both the present life and the life to come.
—1 Timothy 4:7-8

STANDING IN LINE

OH, WHEN THE saints go marching in…oh, when the saints go marching in…Lord, how I want to be in that number…when the saints go marching in."

And they won't be standing in line! The doors of heaven will be open so wide that we will all march shoulder to shoulder, with no waiting, no VIP lines, no X-rays, no puffing machines, and no strip-searches. We will have absolutely nothing to hide. Our sins will all be washed away, and we will walk confidently to the throne of God—to remain there with Him forever!

We will finally be home.

Blessed are those who wash their robes, that they may have the right to the tree of life and may go through the gates into the city.
—Revelation 22:14

EPILOGUE

I RECENTLY ORGANIZED a special event at our Tree of Life Community in San José, Costa Rica, to discuss with my brothers some of the challenges and problems faced by Christians who travel frequently because of business and to pool together our experiences and ideas about the topic. We put together a few Scriptures and recommendations that, while being particularly relevant to the frequent traveler, should also be useful to any Christian who wants to guard his or her heart. Although I acknowledge the limitations of having discussed this issue only with men, I thought it would be worthwhile sharing some of our thoughts with you.

Dealing with the Trials of Business Travel

What does God want from us when we face the trials of business travel?

First, He wants us to have hope. James 1:12 reads, "Blessed is the man who perseveres under trial, because when he has stood the test, he will receive the crown of life that God has promised to those who love him." Which is better: temporary relief from temptation or the crown of eternal life?

Second, He wants us to be aware of danger and of the resources we have at hand. In 1 Corinthians 10:12-13, Paul tells us, "So, if you think you are standing firm, be careful that you don't fall! No temptation has seized you except what is common to man. And God is faithful; he will not let you be tempted beyond what you can bear. But when you are tempted, he will also provide a way out so that you can stand up under it."

Third, He wants us to fast and pray before we go on difficult trips. At a very difficult time for His disciples, Jesus told them, "Watch and pray so that you will not fall into temptation. The spirit is willing, but the body is weak" (Matthew 26:41).

Fourth, He wants us to stay alert and use the weapons we are given. In 1 Thessalonians 5:7-8, Paul states, "For those who sleep, sleep at night, and those who get drunk, get drunk at night. But since we belong to the day, let us be self-controlled, putting on faith and love as a breastplate, and the hope of salvation as a helmet." Paul also tells us in Ephesians 6:10-18:

> *Finally, be strong in the Lord and in his mighty power. Put on the full armor of God so that you can take your stand against the devil's schemes. For our struggle is not against flesh and blood, but against the rulers, against the authorities, against the powers of this dark world and against the spiritual forces of evil in the heavenly realms. Therefore put on the full armor of God, so that when the day of evil comes, you may be able to stand your ground, and after you have done everything, to stand. Stand firm then, with the belt of truth buckled around your waist, with the breastplate of righteousness in place, and with your feet fitted with the readiness that comes from the gospel of peace. In addition to all this, take up the shield of faith, with which you can extinguish all the flaming arrows of the evil one. Take the helmet of salvation and the sword of the Spirit, which is the word of God. And pray in the Spirit on all occasions with all kinds of prayers and requests. With this in mind, be alert and always keep on praying for all the saints.*

Pilgrim's Promise

As we read in 1 Peter 2:11, "Dear friends, I urge you, as aliens and strangers in the world, to abstain from sinful desires, which war against your soul." In Hebrews 11:13, we also read the following about Abel,

Noah, Sarah, and Abraham: "All these people were still living by faith when they died. They did not receive the things promised; they only saw them and welcomed them from a distance. And they admitted that they were aliens and strangers on earth." *We are indeed pilgrims—aliens and strangers in this world—but even more so when we are traveling.* And given the fact that so many people in the Bible were able to live as pilgrims, shouldn't we make every effort to do as well?

At Tree of Life Community, we made a public commitment to guard our hearts, apply the traveler's principles of practical wisdom (see below), bring things out in the light with our pastoral leader, and fast and pray. We called this our "Pilgrim's Promise." As Christians who want to love, honor, and obey God, we commit to doing the following:

1. **Guard our hearts.** We will pray, read our Bible, and stay close to our family even when traveling using regular telephone, e-mail, or Internet videoconferencing services for regular communication.

2. **Live in the light.** We will each have a "guardian"; a close friend who is always fully aware of our battles and difficulties and who will take care of us at all times. Both we and the guardian will be responsible for guarding our heart. We will share with our guardian both before and after the trip about the expected challenges and the ones we actually faced. No secret battles will exist in our lives.

3. **Pray and fast.** We will pray and fast before each trip. We will make sure our small group always prays over us before and during each trip.

4. **Apply the principles of practical wisdom.** We will stay away from, or be particularly careful around, difficult environments such as late dinners, celebrations, long trips, TV sets in the bedroom, or bad company. We commit to being even more cautious during travel than we are at home. Specifically, we commit to the following principles:
   - *Praying every day.* Praying each night after returning to the hotel room allows for special grace and provides time

for digestion after a meal. It is also helpful to have a good Christian book to read.

- *Preparing an agenda on the first day of travel or even earlier, the same way we would at home.* This agenda should be negotiated with hosting colleagues to leave room for rest, exercise, and prayer.
- *Ensuring enough rest.* This may mean declining an invitation for a special dinner or other event.
- *Always having a good book at hand.* Having a good book available will help make good use of down time and shut the door on the enemy.
- *Immediately upon checking in, negotiating with guest service or housekeeping to disable anything that might make us stumble.* This could include a TV set, the mini-bar, or Internet access. Sometimes this can be arranged even before the trip.
- *Exercising at least 15 minutes every day.*
- *Avoiding long trips or travel over the weekend as much as possible.*
- *Not dancing with other women.* ("I only dance with my wife.")
- *Carrying phone numbers for friends or church contacts in each city we visit.*
- *Leaving a copy of our tentative agenda with our family, including phone numbers that allow our wife/husband to reach us anytime.*
- *Protecting the days before and after the trip in order to have a special, peaceful time with the family.*

I would be honored to receive comments and suggestions from you to expand these recommendations. My e-mail address is pilgrim2hvn@gmail.com.

—**Luis Fernando Aragón**

ENDNOTES

Journey 12

1. C.S. Lewis, *Mere Christianity* (New York: HarperCollins Publishers, 2001), p. 132.

Journey 19

1. H. Elliott, "NBC Nightly News to Feature American Baptist Ministry," 2006. http://www.abpnews.com/index.php?option=com_content& task=view&id=1697&Itemid=119 (accessed August 2008).
2. CDC National Center for Health Statistics, data brief #1, November 2007. http://www.cdc.gov/nchs/pressroom/07newsreleases/obesity. htm (accessed March 2008).
3. P. Sherrid, "Piling on the Profit: There's No Slimming Down for Companies Selling Diet Products," 2003. http://health.usnews. com/usnews/health/articles/030616/16profit.htm (accessed August 2008).
4. U.S. Centers for Disease Control and Prevention, *Morbidity and Mortality Weekly Report,* 2006, 55:36, p. 1.

Journey 22

1. You can learn more about Servants of the Word by visiting www. servantsoftheword.org.

Journey 26

1. Ravi Zacharias, *Can Man Live Without God?* (Dallas, TX: Word Publishing, 1994), p. 100.

Journey 27

1. The law applied to Costa Rican faculty from state universities who study overseas for a minimum of two years. The car must have a 1.6L engine or smaller, and it must have been registered under the faculty member's name for a minimum of one year.

Journey 28

1. "I Bless Your Name," words and music by Elizabeth Goodine, © Copyright 2004. Wayne Goodine Music/ASCAP (admin. By EverGreen Copyrights). All rights reserved. Used by permission.

Journey 36

1. "Sing Out O Barren One", words and music by Michael J. Keating. © 1978 THE SERVANTS OF THE WORD (Administered By THE COPYRIGHT COMPANY, NASHVILLE, TN) All Rights Reserved. International Copyright Secured. Used by Permission.

Journey 38

1. This was before September 11 and all the security complications that ensued. I do not know if people are allowed to carry a gun in their checked luggage these days, even if it is unloaded and declared to the airline, as mine was.

Journey 39

1. You can find a document with advice on how to stay physically active during travel at the American College of Sports Medicine website. See http://www.acsm.org/AM/Template.cfm?Section=Search&section=19991&template=/CM/ContentDisplay.cfm&ContentFileID=290.

LaVergne, TN USA
19 January 2011
213146LV00004B/5/P